SAD No More

How to Be a Heart-Centered Person in a World That Tries to Crush You

By Faith Storms, LCSW-C

To Beautiful Molly,

How amazing your kind heart is! I am glad to know you.

Keep your heart light shining!

Hugs,
Faith Storms

Introduction

How often are you hurt by others?

How often are you confused by other's behavior or choices?

How often does your heart ache from a lack of connection or a feeling of being understanding by others?

How often do you feel used by others? How often do you feel taken advantage of?

If these events happen to you on a regular basis, this book is here to help you.

In my 20 plus years of work as a counselor and therapist, I've seen a lot of pain and suffering. I have talked to so many folks with hurting hearts. As a heart-centered person myself, these clients especially touch my heart. I have been where they are - where *you* might be now - sometimes where I find myself, yet again.

My personal hurts prompted my own journey of self help, healing, and growth. For many years I relentlessly sought out various methods in an attempt to understand myself, release old pains and patterns, and move forward in healthier ways. Through this process, I gained much healing and insight for myself, as well as greater personal peace. I passed this on to my clients and sometimes my friends if I could. I gravitated to simple easy methods, which I tested on myself and was then able to share with my clients over the past few years. For myself and so many others, these ideas and methods work very well.

Now I want to share what I've learned with a wider audience in the hope of spreading wholeness and greater health to all. In this very broken world of today, we desperately need more peace and healing. I can only reach so many people through my private practice; I want to help as many people as possible find the inner calm my clients and I have found.

I have created a simple acronym to help people remember the three basic steps one must take in order to make a change: SAD. This stands for Stop – Adjust - Do *You*. Each of these steps will be broken down and explained in detail, and exercises designed to help you accomplish each step will be offered to you.

Not all of these ideas and exercises will apply to you. If you find an idea that doesn't resonate for you, or doesn't work for you, then move on to the next idea. Feel free to come back later and read it again. Another day it might make sense, or be more helpful. If it still seems of no use, leave it. Consider this book a storeroom; take only what you need or what works for you from its shelves. This journey is all about *your* well being.

For myself, I find that different techniques are more helpful at certain times, less so at others. There are times that one method may do nothing for me at all. I think this is typical for many of us due to our shifting emotions. This is why I believe we need a variety of tools in our toolbox. I like to have many options myself, so I teach my clients a wealth of ideas and methods too. This is how I ensure they have the right tools to work with in any given situation.

Change *can* happen - you *can* get stronger - you *can* feel better. It doesn't matter how long you've struggled. It doesn't matter how long you've been stuck. Together, we can get you *unstuck*. I've helped many people move forward in their lives, and I'm confident that I can help you, too.

As I worked on this book, a part of me wanted to share my personal journey, my personal struggles, my personal issues, my personal victories. I do this to a degree in my counseling work. Then I paused and wondered: *What will people think? Will they judge me (badly)? Will they think less of me for some of my choices, for some of my life experiences?* And then I would feel afraid. What if sharing personal things hurts my credibility as a professional? I struggled with this issue from the first moment I started writing.

Choosing to share oneself is scary; even *terrifying*. Choosing to be open, to be vulnerable, is hard. We all fear rejection and we often assume we'll receive it before we even begin. It takes a leap of faith to be transparent, and I'm choosing to take that leap of faith with you by sharing some of my personal journey.

If you study *therapy outcome* literature, the most powerful factor in creating change is the therapeutic relationship itself - how you feel about your therapist, how connected you are to them, how much you feel they care for you – these things are what matter most. Methods used in therapy are literally not statistically significant, so if this book is to be of good use to you, you'll need to have a connection with me, the author; you'll need to feel that I care. Having a connection requires time and experience; I share my life with you here, so you can get to know me; so that you can see I'm not so different than you.

A sense of *positive expectancy* is the second factor in successful therapy, so I also share my experiences (and the experiences of clients and friends) in order to give you hope. For us to be willing to engage in the work and process of change we have to have some hope, some confidence that maybe we can feel better. We don't need to be completely convicted it will all work, but we do need to have the *hope* it will, or we'll never get started.

The most common question I'm asked as a therapist is, "Am I crazy"? It's often asked in a joking tone, but I feel the fear in the question. The question is a serious one. They fear (we *all* fear) that we are deeply damaged, too full of faults, too weak to be able to be well and happy or to live a good life. We fear we are doomed to be miserable.

I used to feel that way myself. I was sure I was too messed-up emotionally to be of much value in this world. There was a point in time when I didn't want to live anymore. I have been in the pit of depression and despair. But somehow I kept going and you will too. It can get better. You can get stronger.

Let's begin our journey together. Thank you for joining me. Thank you for doing this for **YOU.**

Chapter 1
STOP

It's usually wise to start with the most basic concept. When faced with a stressful, emotionally charged situation, the first thing we should do is *stop*. Do nothing. Say nothing. Make no decisions. Do not allow anyone (even yourself) to push you into action.

Our Brain and How It Works

When we're emotionally upset (sad or mad) we do not think clearly. In a state of moderate to high stress our higher brain functions (like decision making) actually shut down. This is due to survival processes. When under stress our brains believe we are in mortal danger. When in mortal danger we don't need to think, we simply need to fight or flee. Under stress the brain de-*evolves*, going from higher brain mammalian functioning (cortex) to lower brain reptilian brain (brain stem).

A part of our brain, called the ACC (anterior cingulate cortex), is the part that perceives threat. A small, almond shaped brain structure called the amygdala is the integrative center for emotion, emotional behavior and motivation. The amygdala can be thought of as our gas pedal. During stress there is an increased production of cortisol from the hypothalamus. This increased glucose (sugar) to fuel the fight or flight response. Our sympathetic nervous system is what ratchets up when we perceive a threat; this system is about tension. These structures are in the brain stem, the older part of the human brain (reptilian brain). When we're in that mode, we often stop using sensory input and instead use past experiences to make present decisions. In the case of a person who's an abuse or trauma survivor this can lead to continued traumatization (if they adopted negative behavior in order to survive in the past).

To be able to make good decisions now, in our present life, we must activate our parasympathetic nervous system. This system is about relaxation, peace, and calm. This calm state of mind is present when different parts of our brain are engaged; the neo-cortex, frontal lobe and temporal lobe. As the psychologist Fritz Perls used to say, "lose your mind and come back to your senses." When we are grounded in our present senses and the more advanced parts of our brain are running the show, we can make better choices.

The goal of self-regulation work is to create just enough physical relaxation to get the client back into their physical body and current situation, and out of their old, automatic fear reactions. We seek to interrupt the sympathetic nervous system and activate the parasympathetic nervous system. You can learn to do this for yourself.

Effects of Stress on Our Body

When we are under stress it changes the chemistry in our physical bodies. One of those changes is increased cortisol production, which in turn decreases our body's ability to reduce inflammation. This means we don't heal as well and fall ill more often. Digestion slows so we have dry mouth and constipation. Our hearts beat faster, so our blood pressure goes up.

With continued stress, the amygdala is stimulated which sets you up for anger and fear. Ongoing stress puts your body into crisis mode. In this mode, your body's resources get hijacked from long term positive efforts (strong immune system, good digestion, even mood) to short term crisis management (which is not based on any *real* threat). All of our major systems are affected by stress; gastrointestinal, immune system, cardiovascular and endocrine are all compromised.

Effects on Our Memory and Mood

Over time, stress creates a more sensitive amygdala. This means we are more reactive, which makes our danger alert system more sensitive. In turn, being more sensitive makes us more reactive. As our alert system is activated more often, our feelings of anxiety climb. While we may worry over specific things at first (state anxiety), over time, we can develop general, ongoing, free floating anxiety (trait anxiety).

I see this a great deal in my therapy practice. Many clients come in saying they don't know why they're anxious. They report no specific problems in their lives. They describe life as okay, over all. In many cases small upsets and hurts, while seemingly not dramatic, collectively have worn down their system. Our body can only take so much stress before it begins to break down.

As stress rises we have less serotonin in our brains. Serotonin regulates mood. Less serotonin makes us vulnerable to depressed States of being. We are more prone to feelings of disinterest in our own lives as well as the larger world around us.

I recently read some truly disturbing information in the book *Buddha's Brain*, on the subject of memory. The writers shared that ongoing stress in our lives wears down the hippocampus. This structure in our brain forms *explicit* memories (detailed, specific, recallable) memories. As the hippocampus functions less well, experiences, especially painful, difficult ones, begin to be recorded in our *implicit* (feeling content without specific, recallable events) memory structures. Memories recorded this way will have the distortions created by an amygdala on overdrive; they will be without the details of what *actually* happened to cause the upset feelings. This results in people saying, "so something happened to me, not sure what, can't tell you what, but I am really upset." This continued emotional state of general unease is totally real for the person experiencing it and It can begin to control them.

Some people feel a little upset a lot of the time and don't have any idea why. I hear this a often in my private practice. These folks feel stupid, bad, and even crazy. They know what they're going through makes no sense, that their reactions are extreme. They apologize to me, for wasting my time, for taking up the time someone with *real* problems could be using. I assure them that their problems *are* real; an exhausted brain.

Stress and Suffering

The book *Buddha's brain* presents some really great information on our brain structure, it's functioning, and how this contributes to stress, and thus suffering. The authors say there are three main parts of our brain; reptilian, paleomammilian, and neomammalian. Our cortical brain tissues are complex, conceptualizing and *slow*. Our sub cortical brain tissues are ancient, simplistic, concrete and *fast*. The picture they use of the three parts of our brain is *lizard-squirrel-monkey brain*. We have these three very different ways of dealing with the world.

They go on to explain that our brain has 3 fundamental strategies for survival:

1. Create separateness (me vs. world),
2. Maintain stability (physical and mental)
3. Approaching opportunities and avoiding threats.

If our system perceives a change, then these processes are triggered. Our brains then register distress if one of these survival strategies is needed. Distress and discomfort are our brain's way of motivating us to fix the problem and help our systems return to balance.

Thousands of years ago our worries were about things we could see and possibly do something about. We worried about animals that could injure or kill us. We worried about holes we might fall into, or objects that could hit us and hurt us. As we grew socially, we began to worry about who was near us and whether or not they liked us. Would they remain near us and help us hunt and protect ourselves? Social, and thus emotional, connections became vital to our existence. It was important that your tribe, your family, your clan, let you stay with them. If you were rejected and ejected from the group, your chances of survival went down dramatically. We are wired to desire community with others.

What is the biggest challenge in our world? Things are always changing! That's why we get activated so often. Our brains were designed more for avoiding than approaching. Our minds are Velcro for negative experiences and Teflon for positive ones. To our brain, sticks and stones are more powerful and impactful than flowers and rainbows.

I explain this not to depress you or make you feel doomed, but so that if your experience has been that bad stuff happens to you a lot more than good stuff, you won't think you are just a *bad* or naturally negative person. Yes, there are a minority of humans out there who are very laid back, relaxed, and don't seem upset by much. But that isn't true for most of us, unless we have an extensive practice in meditation! The good news is that while our natural state is to be activated easily, we can change this. Research on the brain has shown that our brains *can* change, at any age, if we do things that create new mental pathways.

How To Change Our Brain

Changing your brain may sound like a huge task, but it isn't that hard to do. Many small, manageable actions can quiet our over-reactive brains. Doing a few of these each day can make a big difference in a short time.

Relaxing your body is the first and most basic way you can begin to change your brain. A completely relaxed body can't be stressed, afraid, or angry. Breath work can be one powerful way to relax.

Take a moment right now to take a big breath. Hold it for five seconds. Now exhale five seconds. Do this again – five seconds inhale, hold it - five seconds exhale. How do you feel? Do it again. Breathe in for five seconds. Hold it for five seconds. Exhale for five seconds. Do it one more time. In five, hold five, out five. How do you feel now? I do this fifteen second exercise a minimum of four times a day. I feel calmer, more rooted in my body. I feel more connected to myself, and more connected to the earth. I feel more grounded. Doing this simple breathing exercise actually activates our *calming nervous system* or PNS.

Diaphragmatic breathing is another helpful method. You may have also heard this called *belly breathing*. The diaphragm is a set of muscles just below your lungs and above your stomach and gut. When we're doing deep breathing properly, we use our diaphragms, and thus our bellies will expand and stick out.

To practice diaphragmatic breathing, sit in a chair with feet flat on the ground, back straight. Place your hands on your belly and watch them as you take a deep breath, do your hands move outward? If so, you are belly breathing. If they don't move you are only shallow breathing from your upper chest area. Practice this a few times a day. You can also lie flat to watch your belly move when you breathe, making this a good bedtime practice.

If you want more visual instruction, I recommend you check out *belly breathing Elmo* video on YouTube from Sesame Street. It's only two and a half minutes long and very catchy! Share it with your favorite child. (I might be watching it right now!)

Here's a fun thing to try. Our lips have many PNS fibers. Touching our lips can calm our bodies! I've been trying this out lately, and it works. Lip touching's calming effect may be why so many people enjoy kissing. So, go collect some kisses to help your nervous system!

A whole-body method for relaxing is called *wet noodle*. Begin by sitting comfortably in a chair and imagining that your entire body is a soft, flexible noodle. Hold that image for five to fifteen seconds. Take a deep inhalation, followed by wiggling and shaking your body as you exhale, then physically collapsing like a wet noodle. Stay in that slumped state for thirty seconds or so, as is comfortable for you. If you start to tense up, begin again with a deep breathe in, wiggle and shake, wet noodle, and relax.

Another physical method is called *progressive muscle relaxation* which is done by systematically tensing then relax (consciously) every muscle group in your body, working head to toe, or toe to head. This takes some time and practice to learn, but can be very helpful in calming and reducing stress. Doing this exercise also helps you become more aware of what tension feels like, and what relaxed feels like, in different parts of your body. Some of us carry chronic stress physically and don't realize we're even tense. Progressive relaxation is an excellent tool to help you fall asleep if you struggle with insomnia.

To begin, sit or lie down on a comfortable surface. Make sure you're wearing comfortable, non-restrictive clothing. Consciously tense the muscles in your shoulders and hold for about ten seconds, then release. Take a moment to bring awareness to what that feels like in your body. Next tense your arms and hands, making fists and drawing your arms up. Hold for ten seconds, then shake out your arms and rest them at your sides. Notice how relaxed your arms and hands feel. Now tense up your torso, stomach muscles, and hold for ten seconds, then release. Notice how it feels to be relaxed versus tense. Now tighten your upper leg muscles, including your buttocks, hold for ten seconds, then release. Take about thirty seconds noticing what a relaxed lower body feels like before continuing. Tighten your lower leg muscles next, including your calf muscles and hold for ten seconds, then release. At this point your entire body should be more physically relaxed than when you started. Remain quiet and notice how it feels to be intentionally, consciously, relaxed in your physical body. Does any part of you still feel tense or tight? If yes, bring your focus to that area, tighten it up, hold for another ten seconds, then release. Taking a deep inhalation as you tense and a full exhalation as you release will also deepen the relaxation for you.

Let me give you one more fabulous *stop* technique; caring for a pet. For those of you with a furry (or maybe not so furry) non-human friend, one of the best things to do when you're upset is to spend some time with them. Animals live completely in the moment, totally in the now. They can help us become more calm and centered. Even watching fish swimming in an aquarium can significantly reduce blood pressure and produce relaxation. The unconditional love and positive attention we get from a pet warms our heart and makes us feel better naturally. Pets need us, and can give depressed people a reason to get up in the morning. Any time I'm upset and need to get it out, I talk to my rabbits and guinea pigs. Just being near them helps me deal with my emotions, and I have a good laugh or cry. I feel safe with them, and know I can say anything I need to say in complete confidence.

You are Fine as you are

The fact is that as sensitive, emotionally wired creatures, we will get upset by things we don't like or want. There's nothing wrong with you for having that initial reaction. Emotions aren't a *problem* until we take wrong action because of them. Feel what you feel. Don't fight what's present. Don't put yourself down for having emotions. They're part of what make you special.

Time really does heal. Let things settle. Let people and situations simmer down. Given even a little space, many situations will become clearer and calmer on their own. A better way to handle or approach the situation or person may become obvious. Your feelings can and should be taken into account, but so you can respond rather than react.

When the level of emotional upset is mild to moderate, a few minutes might be enough for you to calm down. If the upset is higher, or the issue at hand is more complex, then hours, days, or even weeks may be required. Taking more time to contemplate a problem is never going to cause you to make a worse decision. Taking your time will likely make you feel better about the final resolution. No one ever tells me they regret a decision they made over time, but plenty of people tell me the sad stories of decisions made and acted upon too quickly.

Chapter 2

EFT

Another way to *stop* is EFT.

For me personally, EFT has been a sanity saver. It's given me a very fast and effective way to shift my emotions. As my emotions calm down in intensity, I'm better able to make reasonable decisions. I've seen it work this way for many of my clients as well.

EFT stands for *emotional freedom technique*. It was developed many years ago by Gary Craig. It's a simple tapping technique that you can use anytime, anywhere. It's self-administered so doesn't require the assistance of a professional. I think it's vital that clients have effective tools to use on their own, between sessions. While I truly love my work, I'd also enjoy working myself out of a job!

Gary Craig said, "The cause of all negative emotions is a disruption in the body's energy system." Today's science does show us that we are bio-electrical beings. Sometimes, we get a *short* in the system. These blockages then cause a variety of negative emotions and physical symptoms.

You can use EFT on any upsetting emotion (anger, fear, depression, anxiety), any disturbing bodily sensation (headache, stomachache, muscle pain, tightness, or tension), or any upsetting event (past or present). First, pick the *problem* you wish to address, and give it an intensity rating from zero to ten, with zero equaling neutral, calm, or no disturbance, and ten equaling most intense or upsetting. This rating system is subjective; you rate how you feel in this moment. We measure it in the beginning so we can check our progress. As you keep using EFT, you may reach a point that you no longer need to rate issues and can simply jump into tapping. When I first learned this technique I rated every experience and took notes too, just to make sure it worked!

Basic Recipe

What I teach others and use myself is what is called the *basic recipe*. There are many different tapping therapies being used these days. Tapping has become a part of what is called *energy psychology* and is becoming more common now than when I first came across it. I've stayed with the original, so I've not personally experimented with any other tapping methods. The basic recipe works for me and most others. If it is not broke, why fix it?

Step one is called the *set up*. Tap continuously on the karate chop spot while you say the following affirmation out loud; *Even though I have this* _____ (insert your current problem), *I acc*ept *myself*. Say this affirmation statement three times.

Step two is called *the tapping sequence*. Tap at least seven times (more if you like) on each spot. While you tap, say out loud the current issue or problem you are seeking to shift. A few examples would be; *my anxiety, this headache, the car accident trauma*.

Tapping spots:

- Eyebrow
- Side of eye
- Under the eye
- Under the nose
- Chin (crease, not point)
- Collarbone
- Under the arm

Step three is to check back in with yourself about your *problem*. Is it better, worse, or the same? If it's better but still there, do another round or two of tapping. If it's feeling worse, try another couple rounds of tapping. Sometimes we have so much pain inside us that it can get a bit worse before it gets better. If it's the same, try another round and recheck.

I have recorded videos of myself tapping so you can see how to do it and where the tapping points are on your body. You can review these on my YouTube channel;

just look up my name. There are also many other videos on YouTube of EFT, some by Gary Craig, others by independent practioners. I've also posted videos on the Facebook page for this book; SAD No More.

Many people report some relief after just one round. EFT can reduce emotional intensity, increase physical relaxation, give you a sense of hope or peace, or create a little distance from your current problem. For others, it takes more tapping to get measurable relief.

If EFT works for you, I encourage you to tap daily, even several times a day. It may keep your general stress and anxiety levels down. I consider it a part of my daily well-being routine. When tapping at a random times (when there's no big crisis), simply ask yourself what you're feeling at the present moment. Maybe you're tired, or just a bit stressed. The answer to your self-inquiry becomes the thing you tap on. You may not notice a big change, but that is okay. Any amount of relaxation or lessened tension is a good thing.

You can tap on a general issue, even if it's not presently bothering you. You don't have to wait until you're very upset or agitated about it to address an issue. If you get angry often, you could tap on anger even if you aren't feeling angry at the time. If you generally have issues with self-esteem or self-confidence, tap on that even when it's not a current struggle. If the issue is in your system, it will come up again and again until it's truly shifted or released.

You won't create a problem for yourself by tapping on an issue that's inactive. If you experience any resurging feelings while tapping, the tapping will neutralize them. When I tap on my various issues when they're not actively bothering me, I may get a little uneasy while doing the tapping, but nothing major remains when I'm done.

In my own experimentation, I've even attempted to tap on totally false issues or feelings to see if it creates anything new in me. I tried tapping on *I hate my sister* and got no reaction. That's because it's not a real issue for me. Then I tried, *sometimes I get frustrated with my sister and her emotional reactions to me*. That got a mild reaction, since there is some truth to that statement. It's a personal issue of mine to occasionally feel upset that some people don't seem to *get* me. Tapping helps.

Please don't wait for a big crisis to happen before practicing EFT. You probably won't recall how to do it when you need it, if you haven't used it regularly. If this is a brand new idea, as it will be for most of you, you'll need regular (ideally, daily) practice to become comfortable with it. When I first learned this technique, I would often remember it *after* the stress or crisis was over! I decided to practice every night when I went to bed. I'd tap on any emotions or body sensations present, or feelings left over from the day. I typically got so relaxed I went right to sleep. EFT can be a great tool for dealing with insomnia. I've tapped myself to sleep many times.

Pay special attention to any spots that feel especially good when you tap. Notice any place you feel your energy or emotions shift. That may be your *sweet spot*; an area on your body that is especially receptive. Be sure to include that spot often in your tapping routines. It can also be used as a shortcut in a crisis. Tap that point to get some immediate relief. My sweet spot is called the *gamut spot* (the area between the last two knuckles). Tapping there for ten seconds creates a physical sensation in me of warm, peaceful energy that starts at my head and washes down my body to my toes. I use this spot when I'm feeling stressed at a doctor or dentist appointment. I can tap that spot anytime, anywhere, and no ones knows what I'm doing or why I'm doing it. It is a great emergency stressbusting tool.

Notes to Trauma Survivors

For those of you reading this who have experienced trauma, I'd like to share some additional information. First of all, trauma is a subjective experience. It's easy to point to childhood abuse, rape, war, assault, and natural disaster survivors and assume they have trauma. But plenty of other people, who may not have been abused in any traditional sense (heart-centered people in particular), may also carry the effects of trauma. Any situation in which your mental or emotional well-being or integrity is threatened can also leave trauma issues in your system. Childhood neglect and rejection are also very impactful and social rejection lights up the same parts of the brain as physical pain!

Most adults have been thru many painful experiences, which often leave behind residual negative energy. This can manifest as emotions like sadness, anger, or defensiveness, or an unwarranted lack of self-esteem or belief in oneself. There can be physical effects as well, like headaches, pain, soreness, or stiffness. In the case of an accident, there may be actual changes to your body, and negative emotions can intensify those physical issues. Shame and blame are huge factors that must be addressed if healing is to occur. If trauma is the trapping of negative energy (which I believe it is), then we have to find a way to release it. Talking through it will typically not achieve this. Trauma is primarily held in our bodies, so we need a way to release it. EFT can do that for many.

I've worked with many clients who spent years, even decades, trying various therapies with no significant improvement of their trauma symptoms. Traditional therapies tend to be primarily cognitive, which means they focus on the neck up. While there is a mental component to trauma, a majority of traumatic energy is contained in our bodies, not just our emotional states. We need healing methods that can identify and release this emotional and physical energy, and that we can utilize without assistance. This makes EFT a useful healing method to keep in your toolbox.

As a survivor, it's vital that you are kind to yourself, and permit yourself to be slow and compassionate in your efforts to heal. And I believe EFT is a very mild, gentle way to help yourself move through issues, upset and even traumas.

I work with a lot of trauma survivors. In all my years of teaching EFT, I have yet to have a survivor (or any client) triggered by using it. I've never seen it make trauma symptoms worse. I've never seen it set off flashbacks or abreactions. It has either been somewhat helpful or very helpful to survivors of trauma when symptoms arise for them in their everyday life.

Other Ways Tapping Can Help You

I'm currently working on an online course called *EFT - Tapping for Weight Management*. Peta Stapleton, a researcher from Australia, has studied the effects of EFT on health habits. Using an fMRI, it was discovered that tapping sends calming messages to the amygdala. Remember, the amygdala is that part of our brain that alerts us to danger (or perceived danger). Regular tapping normalized it's activation. In layman's terms, this means that people who use EFT regularly are overall calmer and less reactive to stress. For people with food and eating issues, regular tapping appeared to reduce food cravings as well.

The research team also found that tapping reduced cortisol levels (stress hormone) by 24.9% in one session, compared to a talk counseling session which resulted in only a 14.25% reduction. Tapping reduced reported anxiety levels by 62.3% in just ten minutes. There were also significant and lasting effects in reducing specific fears, or phobias.

A few years ago I had a client who began to have a panic attack in my office while speaking to me. I had not yet had a chance to share EFT with her. As I saw her beginning to feel panicked, I asked her to just simply do what I did, and say what I said. I led her through a round of tapping with the focus on the stress and anxiety she was feeling at that moment. Within two rounds of tapping, the panic attack halted. She was still anxious and upset, but able to use the rest of our therapy session productively. I have had other clients who successfully used tapping to head off a panic attack when they are able to recognize symptoms early enough.

I have had clients who suffered with chronic migraines use EFT to stall the progression of pain. While migraines (as well as other medical conditions) can be biologically based, there is also often a strong emotional component to these conditions. The stress or fear of having an attack or flare up of a condition is bound to cause symptoms to become more intense or problematic. Tapping can help to reduce the stress and anxiety about health symptoms one may be experiencing in this moment.

A few weeks ago, I had an established client come in on an emergency basis due to the incredibly high anxiety she had experienced the day before. She wasn't sure what to do, so she called my office and made an appointment. I applauded her for taking this step to take care of herself as I knew it was very hard for her to ask for help. When we met, she began by saying, "I'm going to lose it. I can't do this anymore!" She was clearly very agitated and anxious. I immediately suggested that we do some tapping together. She admitted she hadn't thought of doing this yesterday. We sat and tapped together for three rounds, and she said she felt significantly better, and able to handle the rest of her day and her life again.

I once had a distraught client that I was teaching to use EFT. She tapped on *I am so upset I hurt Lisa*. She was distraught and crying when she began tapping. After one round she said she felt better, which seemed to surprise her. I suggested that we continue, so we did a second round of tapping on the same issue. After the second round, she spontaneously said, "Oh, maybe Lisa isn't even upset. " I told her I agreed with her conclusion. She had been assuming she had hurt this other person, which was a projection, a negative assumption. There was no actual evidence that she had done anything to harm Lisa. Her brain had to get clear of the emotional upset before she could realize this herself. It's so much more powerful when a person comes to their own positive, healthy conclusions. I could tell them many of these facts, but they wouldn't as readily accept them. No one likes to be told what to do! When we come up with our own ideas and conclusions, we're more willing to accept them as true.

I've personally seen EFT help people find healthy resolutions to their issues for themselves. Once emotions settle, we may get insight or answers we hadn't previously considered. With reduced emotional intensity our brains work better so we can solve our own problems. I have said for many years that people have the right answers inside of them already. They simply can't get past the blocks to those good ideas. EFT can help free up our mental, emotional, and physical energy so we can take the actions needed to take us where we want to go.

Surrogate Tapping

Another concept I want to share with you is called *surrogate tapping*. This is when EFT is done for another person, as if their issue is the practitioner's issue. I do this for a majority of my young clients, and have seen positive, sometimes remarkable, shifts in their behavior at home. When doing this with a child I say the words quietly to myself, but do the tapping physically. I might also have them tap with me, but they often don't see their issues. As a therapist, I do, so what I think should be tapped on, may make no sense to the child. So, I generally tap on any identified feelings or issues as suggested by their behavior or their parent's observations.

I've come to believe that a majority of my child clients have issues with anger. So if the child has nothing specific to address, I tap on *even though I get angry I accept myself* on behalf of the child. I ended up doing this several times a day during my workweek, and never felt it created any anger in me.

I recently became aware that there had been a major shift in my relationship with my boyfriend. Things he did (or didn't do) no longer upset me. I was intrigued by this, but figured it must be a fluke. To be sure for several weeks I would check in with myself to see if I continued to feel better. After my little experiment, I could honestly say, "I don't care." I said this not in an angry way (as I had for years), but in a truly neutral way. I have never felt this way before. My pattern had been to hold resentments towards my partners if they disappointed me. The things that would upset me were personality traits or behaviors that had been there since the beginning. They weren't big, terrible things; just personal differences. Still, I would upset myself by taking their behavior personally. No more.

I tried to figure out what had changed. Lying in bed one night, my brain finally put it together; all the tapping I was doing in sessions with kids was transmuting any anger in me! EFT had shifted the negative feelings in me without my conscious intention. I was amazed. I truly didn't know it could work like this.

A client that I shared the idea of surrogate tapping with asked me if it would make her worry more. In answer, I asked her if she wasn't already worried and preoccupied. She easily agreed that she was. I explained that surrogate tapping can't put a new worry in your head since you're simply trying to reduce or eliminate an already existing concern. This made sense to her.

If you want to try surrogate tapping and the person it's intended for is uncomfortable with it, then don't do it in front of them. Do it nearby, but in another room. Simply focus on the person and their issue and begin tapping for them. Remember, though, that tapping together can be truly amazing, if the other is open to it. If not, tap for them anyway. And tap for yourself in connection to them. For example, if your child is feeling stressed, tap on their stress, and then tap for yourself as the parent feeling sad or frustrated that their child is having a hard time. Chances are that everyone will feel a bit better once you're done.

A note to parents: Even if EFT seems to do nothing for your child, it will still help you take a break. Doing EFT for yourself and then for your child creates a natural break in the tension the two of you are experiencing in that moment. It's a healthy *time out* when things get really tense. It also models the wisdom of taking a break and stepping away from a difficult situation. All kids should learn how to do this for themselves.

On airplanes you are told to put your oxygen mask on first, before trying to help another, even your own child. That same principle applies here. Before you can tap for another, you have to be in a good place yourself. If your child or loved one is distressed, calm yourself first. Tap for your personal upset feelings first; then tap for the other person involved.

There are many applications of EFT. I encourage you to find all the ways it can be of help to you and those around you. Keep tapping!

Chapter 3

Adjust

Step two of *SAD* is to adjust. (I can hear the moans and groans already!) A common question that I get asked by clients when I tell them they have to make changes is, "Why do I have to change?" My answer to this is always the same. Who's hurting? Who's suffering in this situation? Is it you or them? If it's you, than any changes you make are for *YOU*. Changes made by you and for you for your peace and well-being.

Accept

A big part of adjusting is being able to accept *all* of our feelings. This may sound simple, but it's a challenge for most emotionally wired people. For much of our lives (maybe our entire lives), we're often told that we're *too* emotional when we express ourselves authentically. We're told to calm down, chill out, take a pill, or be reasonable. This can lead to becoming suspicious of our own feelings, if not downright *hostile* to them. Many of us reject our own feelings and put ourselves down far more than anyone else in our lives.

This has to STOP NOW. Rejecting your emotions doesn't make them go away - it simply forces them deeper inside - they will return, and usually with a vengeance.

Being practiced at accepting your emotions in your present can prevent a future emotional log jam.

Our feelings are our feelings. We feel how we feel. But we react in different ways to the same things. There's no right or wrong way to feel about anything. A wide range of emotional reactions can manifest during common life circumstances.

As clients share their reactions to life and other people, it will usually makes sense to *me*. But they can't see it because they're too close to it. This is why we need other people to talk things through with.

Affiliate

Here is a practical action step for greater acceptance; find others more like YOU. Stop expecting people who aren't emotionally wired to understand your emotions – often, they will not - they may simply be unable to! Expecting them to puts both of you in a losing situation. They'll be confused, so will do or say the "wrong" things; you'll be more upset and hurt; and now you're fighting with a friend or family member.

When a heart-centered person is upset or distressed, they need another heart-centered person to support them. They don't need a logical person to tell them how to fix it; they often know full well what they'll need to do eventually; they're simply not there yet. We don't need our fun-loving friend to make us laugh; it can make us feel like our feelings aren't important. And we sure don't need a competitive person to try to one up us or become bossy (out of their own discomfort with emotions). We need a heart-centered friend, who will naturally say kind and supportive things. Most heart-centered people are big huggers. They'll hold you as long as you wish or need to be supported. They may want to help you make things better, but they'll express it in a compassionate way that will be easier to accept. They are never pushy or mean.

Many of my heart-centered clients find themselves related to, married to, or somehow connected with, many people who are not heart-centered. They feel they must be on guard, and find it hard to express their feelings or ask for support (as they often don't get the support they need, even when they do ask). I always advise them to find more heart-centered friends and the cultivate these connections and treasure them.

They will usually return and tell me what a huge difference that one effort has made to how they feel about themselves. They're no longer the oddly emotional one. They have a circle of friends who feel and react to life very much the same way they do. They feel like they can finally be themselves. They feel affirmed and supported. And all these things are vital for good health.

When you share with a trusted other and they give you feedback or action ideas, still give yourself time to process their ideas. Don't simply take what they say and run with it. Even if they have some great ideas, let those ideas flow through who you are and what you need and want. Let your final words and actions be in integrity with you. Let it be what truly works for you. Let it be what you can live with.

Self Inquiry or *The Work*

When you have an upsetting thought ask yourself questions. Go within yourself for the answers, go to your heart and gut, not your head. Our minds are what make up the stories that distress us. Take your time when feeling through the answers to the questions.

Let me show you how this works with a personal example. My stressful or upsetting thought is "my boyfriend should communicate with me more." (Notice that most of our upsetting thoughts are absolute statements – using should, must, have to or ought to.)

Question 1 – Is it true?

I typically begin my inquiry process being stubborn and saying, "YES, my boyfriend SHOULD communicate with me more! We are in a committed relationship, right? He says he loves me. Aren't you supposed to talk to people you care about?" At this stage, I'm just mad. So I allow myself to blow it out and complain all I need to. Talking things over with myself helps me release negative energy. I would do the inquiry questions by myself while hiking in the mountains of western Maryland. You can also have someone lead you through the questions.

Question 2 – Can you absolutely know it is true?

NO. The eventual answer to this question is always no. We cannot know anything for sure. Our absolute statements about others are always a projection. Be gentle with yourself as you sift through your thoughts and feelings. Keep asking until you feel settled with *no* as your truthful answer to this question.

Question 3 – How do you react, what happens, when you believe that thought?

Oh, I love this question! So, how does it affect me when I believe that my boyfriend SHOULD communicate with me more? First of all, I feel angry. I get upset when he won't answer my texts. I get stuck worrying about why he's not answering. Is there a problem? Is he okay? Maybe he doesn't love me. I have no peace. Sometimes I can't work or enjoy my free time because I'm so preoccupied with why he hasn't answered. I can even make myself physically ill over such things. There's no good that comes from me holding onto this thought.

Side note, do you see how this entire process is about YOU? This is a way for you to find peace within yourself.

None of this is actually about that other person. Keep that foremost in your mind during this process.

Question 4 – Who would you be without that thought?

By now I feel lighter, having answered the first three questions. I'm not as weighed down by this issue or thought. Sometimes I even giggle about it, seeing the silliness of it. So, if I didn't believe my boyfriend SHOULD communicate more with me more, then I could actually focus on the communication we do have. I could be in the present moment, enjoying my work or free time instead of worrying about why he hasn't texted me back. I would be a calmer, happier human being. I could have more peace. If I wasn't so upset, my brain would work better. I might remember that there are good reasons why he hasn't replied, like he is busy at work or driving!

The next step is the turnaround. I take my original statement and make three turnaround statements.

1. My boyfriend should not communicate with me more. Is this as true, or truer, than my first statement? Yes. Maybe the amount he communicates is right for him.
2. I should communicate with myself more. Yes! This is very much true. Maybe there is something I lack that I could give myself rather than complaining to him.

3. I should communicate with my boyfriend more. Yes, this is much truer than my first statement. Maybe he doesn't know what I would like. Have I even told him in a way he understands? And since I'm in control of me, but not in control of him, I could actually speak to him (calmly and constructively) about this issue.

That's how self inquiry is done. The point of the process is to gain peace. Even if you decide to take some action, it will be coming from a place of peace. Mostly, this process has allowed me to challenge my thoughts and emotions and find a more authentic way to be. It's helped me to first accept and then shift and release any negative emotions.

Additional questions I might ask myself are, "Who said that?" or "Where did that come from?". Another question Byron Katie asks is "Can you see a reason to drop that thought?" or "Can you find one stress free reason to keep the thought?" When going through this questioning process, feel free to ask any additional questions that seem useful to you. The point of inquiry is to break the automatic reactions and patterns. We want to come to current awareness, not be ruled by our stories.

Whose Business Is It?

Another important concept I want to share from Byron Katie is her idea of asking whose business something is. She states that there is *my* business, *your* business and *God's* business. My business is my own thoughts and feelings. Your business is your thoughts and feelings. God's business is anything outside human control. So when difficult things are happening, another good question to ask yourself is "whose business is this?" The answer to that one question can shift a lot.

You're feeling sad or mad. Whose business is that? *Yours*. Your partner snaps at you. Whose business is that? *Your partner's*. Your child seems upset. Whose business is that? This one can get tricky for loving parents. The ultimate answer is that it's your child's business. Since you're in a relationship with your child, it's fine to ask them if something is wrong, or if they need help with something. But it's not healthy to take on their upset feelings, or to stress yourself out trying to *fix* whatever's upsetting them (especially if they refuse the help you offer).

Heart-centered people tend to have a hard time staying out of other people's business. It often starts with good intentions. We care so we want to help. But when we're in someone else's business, there's no longer anyone tending to *our* business, to *our* life. No wonder we feel so alone and abandoned. We abandon ourselves for others all the time. We need to return to taking care of ourselves. We need to stay present to *US*.

We have to find a balance in the caring we do. (I'll address this later in great detail.) But for now, just practice minding your own business and staying out of other people's business. Use an inquiry question to keep you focused on *now*.

People Pleasing

Another element of acceptance is to avoid people pleasing. It's not possible to make everyone in your sphere of influence happy. You just can't please everyone, no matter how you wish to. You can't satisfy everyone who wants something from you. There are only so many hours in the day. You have only so much energy. We have to practice letting go of the desire to never be unliked.

It's okay to want to save the world and to want to help everyone; that impulse comes from your big, deep heart. Honor your love for others. Your feelings are always acceptable. Cherish the fact that you're a heart-centered person. This world needs you very much! But it needs you strong and well, not stressed out and burnt out. The only way we are of service to others is if we are well.

This desire to help others at our own expense is called *codependency*. Years ago this became a very popular topic and there were many books written about it. Melody Beattie was a popular writer on this subject, and her book *Codependent No More* was and is a classic in the field.

Wikipedia says "Codependent relationships are a type of dysfunctional helping relationship where one person supports or enables another person's addiction, poor mental health, immaturity, irresponsibility, or under achievement." This is a good definition, but I would add that in supporting the other, you also do harm to yourself. You neglect or abuse yourself and your own well-being.

Treatment for codependency involves helping the person become stronger within themselves by identifying boundaries and then being able to state and keep those boundaries. Codependent individuals tend to give in to other people's wishes and wants even when they are contrary to their own. Codependents need to learn how to stand up for themselves; it takes practice to be assertive, but it can be learned with practice.

Self Compassion

Here's another simple way to practice accepting yourself. It's called *Self-Compassion*, and was developed by Kristin Neff. (This won't be a new concept to anyone who's studied Buddhism.) In her book by the same title, she lays out all her research on why this works. Here, I'll explain how to use her ideas practically. For me, practicing self-compassion every day on my drive home helps me transition from my work day spent serving others and sitting with their pain, to being in my private life. It helps me stay present to myself and all I might be coping with, and gave me a way to shift into a better mode before I got home. In short, it helps me remember to leave work at work where it belongs.

Practicing self-compassion the way I do has three steps. The first step is to acknowledge that you're suffering. *This is a moment of suffering* is the phrase I use. In my early practice, I found this step to be the most challenging for me. I tend to downplay my own obstacles and hardships; I'll tell myself that what I'm going through isn't really that bad. I see my clients do the same thing. But the reality is, when we hurt, we hurt. We don't live other people's lives, we only live our own. Before we can make a shift we must first acknowledge the problem. This step does exactly that.

Step two is called *common humanity*. Here we remind ourselves that pain and challenge is a part of the shared human experience. You don't do this in a harsh *buck up and deal with it* kind of way, but in a more gentle way. When we're upset or hurting many of us tend to isolate. We don't reach out, we don't share, we don't ask for help. We may end up thinking and feeling that we're the only one struggling. The sad reality is that no type of pain or suffering is completely unique to any one person. There are commonalities in our thoughts, feelings, and reactions. Yes, each individual person has their unique experience, but all people experience pain, suffering, love, joy, and loss. Reminding ourselves that all humans suffer gets us out of our isolative thinking (which increases suffering.) Isolation is so painful to most humans that it's used as a form of punishment and torture. This is especially true for extroverts and those of us who crave intimate contact with others.

Step three is to show kindness and compassion to yourself. I had a client get very hung up on this step because she was trying to make it too complicated. Being kind to yourself can be as simple as taking a deep breath. It could mean you stop rushing and instead slow down a bit. Kindness could be something big and special like a spa day, but usually it won't be. If I've had a long day at work, kindness towards myself might be giving myself the night off, from whatever home tasks I had assigned myself that morning. I may give myself permission to watch TV or a favorite movie when I get home. I might go to bed a bit early to read, or spend extra time with my cavies (guinea pigs) and rabbits without guilt.

Here's an example of how I use this method while driving home from work.

I begin by saying (and yes, out loud!) *This is a moment of suffering. It's tough to spend your days listening to painful stories, witnessing abuse, trauma and painful feelings. You feel stressed sometimes. It's okay to feel your feelings. Other professionals often feel the way you do. They also get tired and stressed. You're not the only therapist to feel this way.* I'll ask myself, "How can I be kind and supportive to myself right now? What do I need?" The answer to that question varies day to day. As I speak compassionately to myself, I take deep, cleansing breaths. I may use my wiggle & wet noddle exercise to shake off any negative energy. Sometimes I say what I'm grateful for. I'll think of something positive about my life, or an upcoming event I'm excited about. I may plan something nice for myself later that evening. I often do EFT for myself. I think it's helpful to find an immediate kindness you can do for yourself (and then do it!), because who knows what might be happening when you get home!

Self-compassion has made a huge difference to how I feel about myself and how productive I actually am. Being self-critical doesn't actually help us do better in life. Research shows that the opposite is true. People who practice self-compassion are just as successful and productive, often more so, than self-critical people. If you think about it, it makes perfect sense. How well can anyone do when they have a mean person following them around all day telling them what they *can't* do and how *bad* they are? Yet many of us do just that with our own inner critic. You must shift this to live the best life possible. And luckily, you can.

Every day we have a chance to accept ourselves and be present to our lives. I challenge you to do this today, to do this NOW. Put the book down and practice accepting yourself in this very moment.

You are worthwhile. You are beautiful. You are a good person with so much to offer the world. You are amazing. You are magnificent. You are so cool! I see that in you. Practice seeing it in yourself.

Chapter 4

Personality

Another step in the adjustment process is to ask yourself who you're dealing with. Who are they in character? Who are they in personality? Our biggest mistake is to assume that others are like us in thought, feelings, and actions. This is a very typical bias we all seem to have. On the off chance the person you're dealing with is much like you, consider yourself lucky. Unfortunately, this tends to only happen about 25% of the time. The other 75% of the time, the person you're dealing with will be quite a bit different than you, therefore they'll think, feel, and react very differently than you.

GEMS

So now let's talk about personality. There are many systems out there designed to help us understand people. A few years ago, I came across a system based on a person's primary motivation in life developed by Dani Johnson. I've found this to be a very simple, useful, practical system to better understand others and improve our interactions with them. For more detailed information check her website. I'll give you the very basics of her system here. I'll also share my personal and professional observations of this system in action.

She begins with four personality types, each called a different gemstone. Each gem can be male or female. In this system we each have a primary or dominant gem, and then we also have a secondary gem. Our primary gem is the automatic response we have to people and life. Our secondary gem is other ways we're also more comfortable being and operating in our lives.

Here is an analogy I came up with one day driving to work. Our dominant gem is our home. It's where we live, where we're completely comfortable and at ease. We operate in this realm automatically. Our secondary gem is like our neighborhood. It's nearby and quite familiar. The other two gems are like foreign countries. They are far away, hard to get to, very strange, and hard to understand.

Ruby

Rubies are motivated by competition. They want to win; they want to be in control. They can often come off as mean and bossy. They're often money and possession motivated. They're commonly into status and recognition. They're terrible losers, and not always good winners, either. Compassion does not come naturally to them; they must be taught a measure of it. Their weakness is the inability to work well with others. They can be easily threatened by someone as good as, or better than them in some way. Rubies act like they're right all the time. They're correct maybe half the time.

My personal observation from a psychology perspective is that competitively motivated people seem to be operating out of ego. Due to this, they're generally very strong willed. It's very hard to take on a ruby. They like a challenge, they enjoy a debate; they don't mind an outright fight. Conflict doesn't emotionally distress these folks. I have verified this with numerous ruby clients, both adults and children. A ruby child is by far the most exhausting type of child to parent. They challenge everything a parent says. I've also observed that rubies tend to be erratically emotional. One day they'll argue passionately about an issue. A week later they will literally not care at all.

Pearl

Opposite of rubies are pearls. Pearls are motivated by service to others. They want to help and save everyone; and the whales and trees too. They're naturally kind and tender hearted. Pearls are deeply emotional, and in a very consistent way. Pearls are more of a behind the scenes type of person who does not generally like public recognition. Pearls are worker bees and work horses. Their greatest weakness is an inability to stand up for themselves. They need to learn how to be, and then practice being, assertive.

Psychologically, I believe pearls operate out of their heart space. This is why they're so often run over and crushed by other personality types. Heart energy is wonderful but not always the toughest. Pearls tend to be peacemakers, not wanting to cause problems or conflicts. Conflict is difficult, and frankly, often painful to them so they may avoid it at all cost. Sadly, this allows others who don't mind conflict to more easily manipulate a pearl. In order to survive in this world full of other types, pearls must stand firm and be fierce about healthy boundaries, even if it's very hard for them. Pearl kids are a parent's dream, usually kind and compliant. Pearl kids can be emotionally crushed if they don't have a parent who understands and supports their tender hearts.

Emerald

The next gem is emerald. Emerald individuals are motivated by logic, facts, and information. These folks will often research topics exhaustively. They often have *paralysis of analysis* and will not take action. Emeralds are schedule oriented and very time conscious. They work off of calendars and generally have their personal affairs in good order. Their living spaces are usually very orderly. The downside of emeralds? They're often perceived as cold and heartless. Emotions are simply not a part of how they process life or communicate with others. They can deliver very upsetting information to someone with no apparent awareness of why the other becomes upset.

From my observation, emeralds operate out of mind energy. As such, they can be very strong-minded. They're right a majority of the time and they know it! Emerald kids can come off as disrespectful when they're just being logical. If you ask an emerald to do something stupid, illogical, or unreasonable, they simply will not. This is different than the strong willed defiance you will get from a ruby child. Emeralds are the one type who often need very little to no human connection. These folks can be lone wolves and are really okay that way.

Sapphire

The last gem is sapphire. Sapphires are motivated by fun. These are extroverted, outgoing party type people. These folks have a big need for other people. They make friends everywhere they go. They're very likeable. They're often loud and may dress brightly. The downside to this gem is that these folks live in chaos. They're usually late, often forget things, and can be rather unreliable. To be successful they need to be taught order and discipline.

My observation is that sapphires live from spirit and soul. They often have a lot of energy and lots of creative ideas. Many kids who are dominant sapphires really struggle in the educational system. School was designed by and for emeralds. Pearls comply with school. Rubies like sports so that can be leveraged to get some academic performance from them. For sapphires, there's nothing about school that's fun. Sapphire kids are often diagnosed with ADHD and then medicated. Some of these kids may need that, but I also see that the school system simply fails this personality type. If properly motivated, a sapphire will get all the other kids doing the project and having a fun time doing it. Sapphires are naturally liked so they can often easily get a group engaged. Sapphire kids are fun to live with, but achievement or goals are never their natural tendency, thus they can be very frustrating to parents.

How To Apply This

As you have been reading this, you've probably easily identified many people in your life by the gem they fall under. You may even be having some *ah-ha* moments about yourself. If so, I'm glad. Knowledge can be powerful and very helpful. This information has been so vital to me in my own life. It's helped me interact with others in a more skillful way.

I'm a pearl dominant. Caring for others is literally automatic for me. Being kind and caring is automatic. Going out of my way for others is also automatic. Boundaries have been a challenge for me. I have had to learn that. What helped me learn boundaries was to lean on and develop my secondary gem – emerald. I can be very logic based, even very cold and "heartless " at times. When my soft hearted emotions would become overwhelming or too stressful, I'd simply tell myself to *be an emerald* and practiced accessing those parts of myself. This allowed me to draw from the non-emotional part of myself for strength. This has worked well for me to help stabilize my emotional life more in the past few years.

I'm presuming most people reading this are pearls – dominant or secondary. You're the personality most affected by others. You're the personality most hurt by this world and the people in it. What your other gem is will affect how your heart piece gets lived out.

If like me you have that logical side, you can use it to lean on in tougher times. When you're overwhelmed with emotion, tell yourself to be an emerald. Encourage yourself to be logical. You have that within you. If you have the more fun loving side then lean on that ability to flow better. Practice letting things roll off you. If your other side is strong willed, then go to that place to get a break from the emotions at times. I think by consciously developing your secondary personality traits, you become a stronger, more well-rounded person.

What you also need to know is that personality is inborn and hard-wired. We are born with these motivations. You can't force a child to be a pearl or an emerald. How a child is parented may affect how their personality is expressed, but will not change their basic tendencies. Even if you're not very strong in your secondary traits right now, they are there within you and can be made stronger. You simply need to use that other part of yourself more often to exercise it.

What is most vital is how you approach others. This isn't about you changing the core of who you are. That will never change. If you interact with others as if they're like you, you'll fail to some degree about 75% of the time. We tend to treat others in ways we like to be treated. We approach others in a way that's natural to us. This isn't the best strategy.

When we assume others are like us, we're projecting. Even if you correctly guess some of what is going on with them, you will never know it all. We need to ask questions and communicate with the other, not just run with our best guess.

The truth in every situation is *they are not me*. They will not think or feel as you do. Tell yourself this to break the assumption that they *will* act like you. So often we get *surprised* when person A acts the way they always do! Why is that? Because we wanted them to act differently. Let me just be blunt; they will *never* be different than who they are. Does that sound harsh? Maybe, but it's the truth. Stop projecting your thoughts, feelings, and beliefs on them and you'll be happier.

I bet you think that's a funny thing for a therapist to say. Isn't it my job to help people change? Yes, but…..

Most human beings don't change, or at least not much. Sounds cynical; and perhaps it is. I do believe people are totally capable of change. However, they have to really want to change. They have to take an active part in making behavior shifts. It takes work and effort. Many of the people you have challenges with in life have zero interest in changing. Many do not see any problem with how they act or treat others. They're not troubled or bothered by their choices or lifestyle. It may be very upsetting to others, but they are currently okay with it. If this is the case, they will not change.

How To Approach Each Gem

When dealing with a Ruby, you must be strong, be bold. Many of them have no respect for niceness or kindness. It literally won't register with them. To act from kindness will be like speaking a foreign language to them. They will not get it. If they're acting badly, call them on it. We often hesitate to do so for fear of hurting their feelings. Remember, they're not you! You will probably not hurt them, or not very much.

I had a client who had a very difficult father who she identified as ruby. We discussed how she could better manage her interactions with him and not get so hurt. I challenged her to stand up to him, call him out when he was being a jerk. She took my challenge and returned to tell me what happened. One day he was being really nasty and she said to him "You are being an asshole."

He laughed. He settled down and the visit concluded okay. His feelings didn't appear damaged, and he appeared to respect her more. She had chosen to act like he does, and he got it. He understood and respected her in that moment (where all her years of being nice had gotten her nowhere.)

I'm not saying to start cursing at the difficult people in your life. But what I am saying is to stand up to strong willed people. Power is what they understand, respect, and are attracted to. Do this standing up in a way that is tolerable to you. You don't need to get loud to stand up for yourself. Frankly, I advise you to not scream or yell. It will make you look like you're out of control. Be neutral, but serious and intense. Be prepared to repeat yourself. They may not believe you at first. Hold firm on your stance.

If you're dealing with a logical emerald, you cannot approach them with emotion. You need to do your research and have your information together if you want them to listen and take you seriously. Approach them calmly. They will likely listen. They will not respond well to upset emotions, however. They'll also not like a lot of hype or overly enthusiastic excitement. This simply makes no sense to them. It is certainly okay for you to be excited about something. Just don't make that the main way you approach them.

When dealing with a fun loving sapphire, find the fun. Show them how an event will be a good time. Make sure they know who will be there (hopefully people they like). Let them know if they'll be meeting new people, as they typically enjoy that too.

When dealing with a fellow pearl, we usually want to know if there's a purpose, what the value is, how it could help others. We don't usually take a lot of convincing; a simple request will often do the trick. If you tell us how we can be a help to you personally, chances are we'll be there for you. We don't want to disappoint. If we say no, please accept it. You know you can probably pressure us into it, but we pearls should support each other in setting boundaries because we really know how hard it is for us.

Saying *thank you* can also be tailored to personality in order to make it the most impact and meaningful. To a sapphire a simple "You rock!" will light them up. An emerald will appreciate hearing just how they contributed to the success of the team or project, but in detail. "Your thorough research gave us the information we needed for a successful proposal" would be well received by an emerald. A ruby wants to know they are outstanding, or the best. "You are the best leader our team has had in a long time" would be well received by a ruby. A pearl likes a lengthy, emotional thank you. "You have done so much and mean so much to the team. Your kindness, helping hand, and positive attitude are invaluable to us all. We value you on our team" will deeply touch a pearl.

Knowing who you are dealing with and what motivates them and matters to them will allow you to have the best and most productive interactions. To me this is both smart and wise.

The other day on Facebook I saw this meme – *You save everyone, but who saves you?* It really struck me. I reposted it, adding these words of my own:

That would be ME. I take care of ME. I am responsible for ME. I "save" ME (with the support of the proper help and helpers.)"

I think it's important that we stop blaming others and take responsibility for ourselves. Not in an angry or resentful way, but in a calm, strong way. We can care for us best. We know us best. If we truly embrace who we are, truly accept ourselves, truly love ourselves, we will be a remarkable force in this world.

Chapter 5

Do You

How do you maintain the healthy shifts you've been practicing so far? You do this by taking care of YOU. You do this by making yourself a priority in your own life.

I often get resistance from my heart-centered clients when I encourage them to make themselves a priority, because they're so used to putting everyone else first. Due to this, they're often burnt out, worn out, and feel unloved and unappreciated. While it's great to get love and support from others, we can't count on it. We have to develop ways of caring for ourselves.

Remember, you can't please everyone. No matter what choices you make there will most likely be someone in your life who won't like it or will disagree with you. If you look to others to make you feel okay, you'll be disappointed a lot.

Here's a seemingly simple question: *Who are you*?

What comes to mind? Probably the roles you play. That's what most people come up with. I'm a parent, a nurse, a sister, a brother, an animal lover...any of these may be good things about your present human life, but they're not *you*.

Spirit/Soul Identity

At a deep level we are Spirit, we are soul, we are a part of the Divine. We are each a child of Spirit, a child of the Divine force, a child of God/Goddess. (A note on the gender of Spirit: Spirit is not human. Spirit has no gender. It doesn't matter what we call it.) We need to ground ourselves in Spirit daily or we're in danger of getting caught up in our human struggles. I deeply believe we are spiritual beings having a human experience and not the other way around. We're so much more than the human struggles we go through.

One of my earliest memories is of a spiritual experience. I remember being at a church altar with a big, loving man (the pastor), and light streaming through beautiful stained glass windows. I was becoming a Christian and asking Jesus into my heart. I felt total and incredible love and peace. I knew then that God was real, and in me somehow. It changed everything. Feeling a personal connection to Spirit gave me strength and grounding. It was a strong foundation for me as a child.

As spiritual beings, we need activities and practices that will nurture our spirits. These could be solitary activities, or activities with others. I encourage you to develop some of both.

Prayer & Meditation

Let's start with some solitary activities. Prayer and/or meditation can be very powerful practices to incorporate into your life. Spending time each day quieting the mind and body is invaluable to our health and well-being. Prayer and meditation can change our brainwaves into more peaceful and restful patterns. Alert, working brain waves are called *beta*; relaxed, reflective brain waves are called *alpha*; when we're in a meditative or prayerful state, our brainwave pattern changes to *theta*. Sleeping brainwaves are called *delta*. Alpha and theta patterns are helpful to our health, and with conscious effort we can increase the time we spend in these states.

Prayer time, alone, at the altar of my pastor father's church early in the morning, is a wonderful memory of mine from my teen years. I could really feel God's presence in that holy place. It was so moving, so powerful. I felt so close to God. It was a good way to start my days.

A relaxed and meditative state can be achieved in a variety of ways. Structured times of prayer and meditation are only one way. Many people find that nature helps them to settle into themselves. If you study the lives of mystics through time, many of their transformative experiences happened in nature. Another door to these states for some is singing or chanting, which can also be deeply moving.

Years ago, I took a series of weekend courses on meditation called *Zoetic Meditation,* which was created by Liora Hill. She is an amazing spirit and powerful teacher. I went in with no experience of any kind with formal meditation. The first class taught all the basics, and was very powerful for me.

Doing meditation in a group has a very different feel to it than doing it alone. The energy is different, bigger, more powerful, and for me at least, more cosmic. It's a worthwhile experience to have. In the weeks after I first learned how, I meditated daily and had a wonderful personal coach to support me. Daily meditation helped quiet my mind.

Something unique to zoetic meditation is an exercise called *permission conversations.* I won't attempt to explain it in detail here, as it's a bit complicated, but if it sounds interesting to you, please visit her website (listed in *Resources*). Permission conversation is the practice of identifying issues that you don't have freedom around, or haven't given yourself permission to investigate. Once you identify an issue, you then work through it using a questioning and discussion format until you have peace inside; until you've given yourself permission to feel whatever you feel about the issue.

While taking 20 minutes to do a formal meditation each day may be ideal, research shows that being quiet, centered, and mindful for even 30 seconds still makes a difference in our minds and bodies. Stopping a minute or two several times a day to take a few mindful belly breaths can be so helpful. Anyone can fit that into their day. Anytime you find yourself waiting, use that time to quiet your mind and body and be present with yourself. You'll be better for it, and your day will probably flow better as well.

Personal Passions

Many people find that regularly engaging in a personal passion or hobby is both mentally and emotionally healthy for them. I encourage my clients to have outside hobbies and interests separate from their partners, kids, family, or work. Something that is of service to others is especially satisfying for heart-centered people. Any activity is fine, as long as you gain something personally from it.

As heart-centered people, we need to start to, and then continue to, find balance in our lives. Most heart-centered people put everyone before themselves. What this communicates to your inner self, and also to everyone around you, is that they all matter more than you do. Time is love. What and who you choose to spend time on, determines what is valuable to you. If you never make time for you, it says that *you* do not matter much. And that's how others will treat you.

I encourage my heart-centered clients to balance the scales. I invite them to make themselves and their health as important as everyone else's. This is a difficult task for the heart-centered person; it feels wrong, selfish. But how good can you be for anyone else, if you have a mental or physical breakdown? If you end up in the hospital or simply unable to function at home anymore, how will you take care of everyone who counts on you? Frankly, it's more selfish to completely wear yourself out. If we want to keep being of useful service to others, we've got to learn to take very good care of ourselves. It's hard work taking care of the world! It's hard work to feel so many feelings all day, every day. We need to replenish ourselves on a regular basis.

Relationships

Please don't try to do this all alone. We need one another. We are social beings, made for relationship. *A General Theory of Love* says this about complete independence:

"As the nervous system matures, a baby reclaims some regulatory processes and performs them autonomously.

Even after a peak parenting experience, children never transition to a fully self-tuning physiology. Adults remain social animals: they continue to require a source of stabilization outside themselves. That open-loop design means that in some important ways, people cannot be stable on their own – not should or shouldn't be, but *can't* be. This prospect is disconcerting to many, especially in a society that prizes individuality as ours does. Total self-sufficiency turns out to be a daydream whose bubble is burst by the sharp edge of the limbic brain. Stability means finding people who regulate you well and staying near them."

I adore this quote and share it with as many people as I can!

When are we hurt in life? Are we hurt when we're alone? Are we hurt all by ourselves? Not usually. We're usually hurt when we reach out and are rejected, right? We're harmed in relationships with others, right? We're betrayed within a relationship, right? We're traumatized *IN* relationship, not when we're all alone. Due to this truth, our healing must also come in relationship. I think this is why the therapeutic relationship is the most vital aspect in therapy, if positive change is to transpire.

When I think of the most powerful moments of change, shift, or transformation in my life, nearly all of them included other people. When someone is really present with me, focused on me, accepting of me, and loving to me, I can relax and heal - something big changes inside of me - and then I can take their love for me and love myself a little more.

Of course we need to be okay on our own at times, too. We need enough self-regulation skill that we can get by when our support systems aren't available. But to try to do your whole life alone is biological idiocy, at least for us heart-centered people. I think we might need others even more – but it must be the *right* others – people that are healthy for *us.*

As I was writing this book, I suddenly got discouraged one day and started doubting myself, doubting my ability to write. I reached out to a couple of heart-centered friends. One of them texted me back in less than 30 minutes with some encouraging words; the other, also a writer, sent me a long, encouraging and helpful message about 2 hours later. I have quite a collection of heart-centered friends (many at a distance) that I can text or message anytime, and who will almost always very quickly send me back a loving message that was exactly what I needed. I've tested this time and time again whenever I've faced challenges in my own life, and it always enriches me.

Friendship comes in many forms. Some people see or talk to a friend daily. Others see or talk to friends weekly or monthly. There is no *right* way to do friendship. There's no *right* way to be connected to another. It's whatever works for the people relating. "It's what's in our heart that really matters" my pastor said recently. This is especially true for us heart-centered folks. We can feel love from afar quite well.

Thanks to the Internet and social media your closest friends no longer need to be geographically near you. Many of my dearest heart-centered friends today are people I have met and gotten to know primarily online through my critter hobby. I've been able to meet some of them in real life as I traveled around the country judging cavy shows with with my cavies (guinea pigs), which has been a huge pleasure for me. Our ongoing friendship are maintained online.

Many heart-centered people lean towards the introverted side. As introverts, we're not always in touch consistently. We may not always show up for parties. We really don't like small talk. But we're here when needed, and respond instinctively from our hearts.

This is precisely why heart-centered people need to find other heart-centered people and then cultivate relationships with them. Here's how I suggest you do this. When you're in a good place, when you have the time and energy, reach out to your heart-centered friends and put some emotional deposits in their love tanks. Send a kind message. Do something nice thing for them. It doesn't take much for it to be meaningful to a heart-centered person. By taking small but loving action, you build good will, a smart investment. When the day comes when you need a listening ear or a helping hand, the friends you have invested in over time will be quite happy to return the favor.

When we're having a tough time we often hesitate to reach out. We don't want to be a bother. But how much do you really need? We seem to fear we'll take up too many hours of someone else's life. Do we really? Do we ever? The most truthful answer probably is *rarely* or *never*. When I'm having a *moment*, what do I actually need? A few compassionate texts can change everything. A few minutes with certain people on the phone, a kind posting or tagging on Facebook, can make such a difference to me. Little things mean so much to heart-centered people. The saying *It's the thought that counts* was probably spoken by a heart-centered person.

Community is often vital to a heart-centered person. Your community can be a church or spiritual group. Meeting together with like-minded others can be nurturing to your spirit. It also meets some practical needs for companionship and help. Other times, a community might be like minded individuals who unite around a cause or ideology. These can also be helpful to a heart-centered person. Some people find their tribe by getting involved in a personal interest. Hobby groups sometimes become very much a second family. Remember our limbic brain? We *need* others in our life; period.

Self Care

When it comes to caring for ourselves, there's a neat approach called self parenting that I discovered in my twenties. Deficiencies in our actual childhoods can't be completely undone, but self-parenting methods can do a lot to mitigate the existing damage and begin to create a better connection to ourselves. *Self Parenting: The Complete Guide to Your Inner Conversations* by John K. Pollard discusses the inner dialogue we all have with ourselves. We all have an inner parent (often critical), and an inner child. The inner child is where our energy and motivation comes from. If the inner child is not being cared for and tended to, it may try to sabotage the adult's efforts to do life and get things done. We become at odds with ourselves. The key is to create productive inner dialogue in order to create win/win outcomes, and get everyone's needs addressed.

Here are a few more simple and practical ways to strengthen and nurture your inner child. One fun way to practice self-care is with adult coloring books. These have recently become very popular. Last Christmas eve

 I was at the grocery when I spotted an animal themed adult coloring book at the checkout. Impulsively, I bought it for myself. The next day I received a nice set of colored pencils for a Christmas gift. When I sat down to do my first coloring session, I actually had a mild headache. I did the coloring anyway. I found that in a few minutes, not only did I feel calmer, but my headache was actually better. I'm finding that coloring is a very nice self soothing tool that can be done for just a couple of minutes or all day long!

I did some online searching to see what was making adult coloring books so popular, and actually helpful. What I found was that there were several factors at play. Coloring has a pleasant association to happy childhood times for most people. Coloring is also a low risk activity, as there is truly nothing to lose, and therefore little stress. Things that are low risk help our brains enter mindful, meditative states. When we engage in a simple yet predictable activity, it creates mindfulness. Being in *mindful mode* induces the theta brainwaves that are so good for us.

Another great practice is gratitude. This practice is taught and promoted by many people these days. Way back when, I remember Oprah discussing it on her show. *The Secret* by Rhonda Byrne recommends it as a daily practice to help create a better future for yourself. Many inspirational teachers past and present recommend this practice as well. Gratitude practices can be very simple. Once a day state or write down three things you are grateful for in your life. These three things can be tiny or huge. What they are is not important. Changing our focus from the stress you're feeling, to what's going right, can shift your attitude. It changes how we feel. It changes how the world feels. It changes your energy for the better, making it more positive and higher in vibration. Some people keep written gratitude journals. If this appeals to you, then I suggest you try it. More technology based people can set an alarm on their phones to remind them to stop and take stock of what they're grateful for that day. Even better, if you have a family meal at your house, invite each member of the family to share something they're grateful for. Let it become a nightly family practice.

I want to touch on the subject of medication. People have a variety of opinions on whether it's a good idea or not; I get it. Nothing's perfect, nothing fixes everything. Some people can make life changes mostly on their own, with good support and decent therapy or self-help. Other folks, no matter how hard they try, can't make positive changes without it. Their moods are too extreme, their behavior too erratic. They literally cannot be productive or happy in their natural state.

There are mental health conditions that have a biochemical basis, such as psychotic disorders (schizophrenia), many depressive disorders (such as bipolar disorder), and many anxiety disorders. Many people with these issues need chemical assistance to be able to live a good and productive life.

I seem to be one of these people. I've been on antidepressants in the past and they helped me. Last year, I fell into the pit again, for no particular reason. Everything in my life was stable, no recent changes, no big problems. It had to be biochemical. I fought it off for weeks. One day I realized it was interfering with my work. That was the final straw. I went to my doctor and went back on the medication that had helped me before. In three weeks or so I felt much better. Yet I still had some internal judgement about taking a pill! I'm a professional for heaven's sake! But I am still human; I'd would rather not have to take a pill.

Last summer, as I struggled with whether or not I should be taking medication, I asked myself some questions. *What is the wise thing to do? Is it wise to suffer when there's a cure? Is it wise to suffer when there's something that I know will help me? No, it's not wise to suffer. It's foolish.* The truth was, I would never ask a client or friend to suffer when there was a possible solution available. So I chose self compassion and continued to take my medicine.

For several months I took a pill every day and functioned very well. After 8 months or so, when I was feeling much better, I decided to stop taking it. It was the *totally* wrong thing to do, of course, especially in winter. After about three and a half weeks off of it, I could feel my mood slipping. My obsessiveness was returning. So I went back on my medicine.

Heart-centered people often get overwhelmed with all the need and pain in the world. We want to help; we want to make a difference. It can be painful for us to witness suffering that we feel we can do little about, such as fundraising commercials or news showing pictures of starving children or abused animals. Those commercials can literally hurt us, as can scary or violent movies can. When we see such big pain, we need to scale it back and focus on what we *CAN* do to help. We need to consistently do good deeds and then focus on what we *are* doing, rather than all that you think is left to do.

What we do matters to the person or being we're interacting with. I once read a story about a small boy tossing beached starfish back into the ocean. A man told the boy that there were just too many, that he could never save them all, so what he was doing wouldn't matter. The little boy tossed another starfish back into the ocean, and turned to the man and replied, "It mattered to that one. "

None of us can do it all, and we shouldn't even try. We only need to do what we can. Each life we touch touches many others. We're better for doing a good deed, even if only for a single person. Our actions are ripples in a pond. Remember the movie It's *a Wonderful Life*"? I watch it every Christmas and always cry, believing in its message a little more than before. We each matter so very much. We just have no idea how much.

Chapter 6

How to Raise a Heart-Centered Kid

Some of you reading this may be either raising a heart-centered kid, or know one. Your sweet, compassionate kid is a joy to parent. This child is so easy, usually doing the right thing all on their own. They're typically obedient and kind, and if they do make a poor choice, they'll often tell on themselves. They're generally not very good liars.

The Lost Child

As heart-centered kids are truly easier to parent, they can often get lost in the shuffle of life. They're rarely the squeaky wheel in the family. Other kids, with louder issues and behaviors, will demand parental time and attention. If there are no other siblings, the noise of life and other demands on the parent may take precedent.

Parents don't usually purposely neglect a heart-centered kid, it just tends to happen. This is in part due to the natural tendency of a heart-centered kid to not want or need the spotlight. They often don't want to be the center of public attention. They also will rarely create chaos to get parental consideration. They don't like conflict; they don't want anyone to be upset with them. Since they rarely make waves, they may get put to the side or put off. Parents may not notice that their sweet kid is *not* just fine.

I'm not saying that all heart-centered children have emotional issues, but they are more vulnerable. Living in this harsh world with such a tender heart is hard. Kids are not born knowing how to live with and manage their feelings. They need to be taught how to do that in a healthy way. They need to be guided and gently supported if they're to become their best. They need help to become stronger.

Truthfully, a heart-centered kid will never require as much blood, sweat and tears as your stronger willed kids. Heart-centered kids need a gentle, supportive, emotionally wise guide to teach, model and support them. They need a caregiver who will take the private time to talk about feelings with them. Heart-centered kids need to be told that all their emotions are okay. They need to be told that all feelings are normal. When they learn to accept their own feelings they can begin to move through their various emotions with confidence.

What Do They Need?

I was talking to my brother-in-law about his very kind-hearted son, my nephew. He was telling me that he thought his son needed to learn how to be tougher if he was going to make it in the world. I hear this a lot - the idea that you have to make these kids *hard*. I completely disagree with this approach. Let me tell you why.

First of all, it won't work! You cannot change a person's internal wiring. Think of a time when someone tried to change YOU. How did that work out for them? I bet it didn't. Or if you did *change*, it was only temporarily.

Secondly, trying to force someone be what they're not sends them the message that they're not acceptable as they are. The rejection of who they authentically are is painful. This is not the way to motivate someone to do things differently. Change begins with acceptance of who they are in the present.

As I told my brother-in-law that night, the answer isn't to make our heart-centered kids tougher, but to teach them to be wise and discerning. They need to learn how to know who to trust, rather than being told to stop trusting everyone. They need to learn how to know who to lean on, rather than never asking for help at all. They need to be taught to be assertive in order to take care of themselves, but in a way that respects the kind souls that they are. They *WILL* be hurt as they learn all of this; they will need a wise parent who can be present to their hurts, offer them support, avoid blaming or shaming them, and generally help them to find the better way to handle hurtful situations.

It's normal to want to rush in to protect these kids. It can be easy for momma or poppa bear to want to champion them. And sometimes that's okay, especially in cases of serious threat. However, rushing in to fix things all the time can communicate to your child that you don't think they can handle life.

They may jump to the conclusion that you think they're weak, helpless, or unable to keep themselves safe. Most parents aren't trying to relay this message to their child; they're simply trying to help. As parents our job is to prepare our children to be productive, healthy adults. You, the parent, will probably leave this earth before they do, so they will need to be self-sufficient. They'll need to be able to take the lead in their lives. They can always request assistance, but they'll have to be able to do things for themselves.

Parents who rush in can overwhelm the rather quiet heart-centered kid. As you protectively declare what needs to happen, or what must be done, that loud energy coming from you may very effectively shut your child down. They may not have the strength to stand up to you, to speak up. Remember, they don't want to upset or disappoint you. It is okay to want to be the bear protecting their cub, but we need to pull back on the intense energy sometimes, to make a space for our quiet child.

Communication With A Heart Kid

Another thing to keep in mind is that a heart-centered person is not always ready to talk when you're ready to listen. Heart-centered people often need time to sit with their feelings before they're able to try to talk about them. Due to this reality, don't be surprised if your heart-centered child denies needing to talk about anything, or deny being upset, even though it's totally clear to you something's going on! As long as there's no immediate danger, give them time. Let them know you're willing to listen whenever they are ready to share.

As a therapist, I would also encourage you to explain to your heart-centered kid that they don't have to tell you *everything*. Let them know that they can talk to you about as much of the situation as they wish to, and that you'll respect their privacy. Each person is entitled to privacy, even children. I think this is vital to gaining a person's trust. But it must be true! Please don't tell your child you respect their privacy, and then go behind their back in some way. You will destroy any chance of being trusted and having a close relationship. If there's a safety issue, be up front and honest with your kid. Tell him exactly what worries you. Give them details. Give them a chance to tell you what's going on for them. Sure, you have every legal right to go through their things, but this should never be done behind a child's back. Kids should be told up front that if there is *just cause* for a search, they will be informed and present when it occurs. This models respectful behavior, while doing things behind a kid's back models sneaky behavior. Don't be shocked if your kid becomes even more secretive if you employ such tactics. If you want your children to be honest with you, then you must be honest with them. You're the adult; you set the tone and pace in your home. Kids do what *we* do, not what we *tell* them to do.

My son Luke is primarily a heart-centered kid (fun loving secondarily). There are times I feel like something is going on with him, but when I ask he'll say he's just fine. Now, he just turned fourteen, so that's a pretty typical adolescent response. Here's what I do. After the first *nothing* response, I'll say to him," I really feel/think something is wrong/going on with you. Will you tell me? " If he still denies an issue, I'll just say, "Okay, I won't keep asking. I do think something's going on with you, and if you want to talk about it later, I'm here for you." Then I literally leave him alone. I don't keep bugging him! It's now up to him if he wants to share with me.

I understand that my son's feelings are HIS business. If I'm concerned about him, I express that to Luke directly and with kindness. That's my part in our relationship. I can't make him talk, and I don't want to anyway. I want him to share with me because he feels safe and comfortable. This is the kind of connection I've created with him over the years, so he actually does talk to me about a great deal. I'm honored and glad about that.

He talks to me only when he's ready to. I accept that. This is why we need to spend time with our children every single day – to create opportunities to connect and communicate with them.

It's not very hard to get a heart-centered kid to talk; be quiet, be gentle, be kind. Show interest in them. Show interest in what matters to them. Show them that you care, that you like them, and they'll like you right back by opening up to you. Heart-centered kids are easy to like. I so love each heart-centered child I've ever had the privilege to work with. I get them, accept them, treasure them, and they feel it and blossom.

Heart-Centered Children's Relationships

When your heart-centered kid has been hurt by someone, resist the urge to tell them to dump that person as a friend. Don't trash talk about the other person. Your child may still care for or be attached to them. You want to ask them open ended questions to help them think through how they wish to handle the situation. Ask them questions like, *When did this happen? Who said that? What happened next? Where did this happen?* Avoid asking *why* questions.

After you've listened for a time, ask them if they would like your input. Don't give them your input unless they agree. Then present your reaction and feedback in the form of suggestions, ideally more than one, so they have several to choose from. Support them in their choice, even if you would have chosen differently. This is their life and their journey. Tell them you believe in them and their ability to handle the situation. Let them know that we all have struggles and we all make mistakes. Let them know that changing plans or strategies is just fine. Take the shame out of *failure*. Reframe perceived failures as a learning experiences.

The heart you hold in your hands is a precious one when you have a child in your life. A heart-centered child has much to give to the world. You can help them be their best by being a great example yourself. You being a *strong* you is what they need most.

Chapter 7

Expanding You

By now I hope you've gained some new ideas and a few helpful new skills. Let's expand on this even more. You deserve the very best life possible. You deserve to be the best you possible! You deserve to be who you want to be. And you can. I believe that for you.

Get Physical

We all live in physical, human bodies. I realize some of you wish you didn't for all kinds of different reasons. Some of you have been physically or sexually abused, your bodies violated and betrayed by those you loved and trusted. It can be hard to heal from that. It can be hard to feel at ease in your own body again. Some of us have just never felt at ease physically. We live more in our heads, in our minds, in our imagination.

To be the most and best we can be, I think it's important to be in connection with your physical self. How can you do this? Movement is one way.

I was never athletic. I had very serious asthma as a small child, so I was the book worm kid, always reading. I never felt coordinated. As a young adult, I figured I should be more active by doing some form of exercise. I had never been a gym person, not into sports, definitely not into dancing. Then one day I overhead a friend mention to another friend that she could show them some belly dance moves (they wanted to go to a Halloween party as a belly dancer). I was intrigued. I'm sure I would have never attended a belly dance class taught by a stranger, but I knew Alix, so I tried it.

It was fun. It was different. I liked that. I managed to do all the moves with some practice. Some moves were simple, easy, and even enjoyable. While men do eastern dance, my classes never had any males, so I got girl time. I took classes for years. That weekly class time was special to me. I even continued to do belly dance while pregnant with my son. Many eastern dance moves can help prepare the body for labor. Alix told us how she used dance to help her thru labor when birthing her children.

Finding something to do that involves moving your body is very healthy. I encourage you to pick a sport, hit the gym, or go dancing. If nothing else, go for a walk. When I lived in western Maryland I would hike in Greenbrier State Park. It was helpful physically, and emotionally, and spiritually. I worked through many issues in those woods. Nature is very healing to me. Find an activity you actually enjoy to some extent, or you'll never keep it up.

Gabrielle Ross explains that in many shamanistic societies if a person is depressed, sad, or non-functional they, will speak to the shaman. The shaman will ask a series of questions: *When did you stop dancing? When did you stop singing? When did you stop being enchanted by stories? When did you stop enjoying the silence?* Clearly singing, dancing, stories, and silence are all part of what helps to keep us mentally and emotionally well. And when stress comes, these activities are often the first to go.

My Personal Spiritual Journey

When I moved to southern Maryland, I was fortunate to find a wonderful belly dance teacher in Karima (Karen Marshall). Her weekly classes became a safe haven for me. Her gentle, kind spirit led to amazing soulful classes. Not only did I get to move my body, but my heart and soul were fed too.

Taking dance lessons from her led me to see a flyer for energy healing work by Shellie Lambert. I had always been curious about energy healing and how it all works, so here was a chance to explore. In our sessions I could definitely see and feel energy shifting in my body. It was very helpful in many ways. She also shared information that she was receiving from her angels and guides. I was never into angels or guardian angels myself, but I listened to the information and much of it was interesting and some of it was helpful.

During this time I had grown increasingly disenchanted with Christianity, though my relationship with Jesus had gotten me through growing up into early adulthood. I began to explore other ideas, even though I was still attending my protestant Christian church on a regular basis. I felt like there was more for me.

Animals and nature were always of great interest to me. The idea of animal guides or animal spirits was enchanting. I bought a book on animal guides and talked to Shellie about how this might work. The book instructed that if you wished to find out who your animal guides were, there was a ceremony you could do to help you discover them. I followed the instructions, doing exactly what the book said to do, and got absolutely nothing. No animal came to me, no impressions came to me; I got no information or guidance. It was frustrating.

A few weeks later as I sat in church, I suddenly became aware of what felt to me like an eagle flying above my head. I was surprised by this of course, but I knew the eagle was a very strong spirit animal. I remember thinking *I don't want to pretend to be more than I am.* I heard a voice saying *You can't be less than you are.* That shut me up, and I simply accepted the presence of this eagle spirit. It stayed with me, and remains with me to this day. Anytime I focus on the area above my head, I feel/sense the eagle flying.

In the spring, I discovered an owl that had been hit on the road near my house. Sadly, he was dead when I found him. I felt moved to take his body back to my house and remove the wings to keep. A few weeks afterwards, I was driving to a cavy show when I suddenly felt an owl spirit fly to my left shoulder while I was driving and land there. I do believe that spirit was the owl I had the wings from. The owl guide has also continued to be with me since that day.

The following winter, as I was doing some healing and introspective work, I became aware of a bear, or more accurately, a family of bears, which felt to be behind me. I always have been kind of interested in and drawn to bears, and now it was clear that they *had my back* and were always around me. I took great comfort in their strength and quiet power. I needed that in my life. They were very grounding for me.

While I was doing this energy healing work and discovering my animal totems, I also went ahead and took some Reiki training that Shelly offered. The training was very good at opening up more levels of awareness for me. I was told that I *ran energy* without realizing it when I touched and massaged others.

About this time, I also became aware of the presence of a special rabbit from my childhood who stayed around my feet. This meant a lot to me.

While I was never really interested in angels, I became kind of curious to see if I had any around me. Shellie assured me that I did, that we all do, that but you couldn't usually hear or feel them. One day I decided to simply try to tune in and see if I could sense anything. What I eventually discovered was that I do seem to have two angel spirits who are with me at all times. On my right I have a very strong female warrior angel, and on my left I have a male angel figure. This was fascinating to me and became part of my ongoing analysis of myself and my issues.

What This Means For You

Here's a huge take away from all my years of discovery; I am *NOT* alone. So many of us feel so alone much of the time. We may not have the friends we wish, the partner we wish, or the family we wish. This can make us feel very isolated. As I was exploring my animal guides and angels, what I ended up feeling is that I'm never truly alone. And I think that is the biggest truth and reality that came out of all those years of searching. Whatever we may call the spirit or spirits around us, the bottom line is that we are never alone. We need to remember this and rest in the knowledge that we are loved, and that we're supported by a higher power(s).

I realize that some of you may think that this is all goofy nonsense. And you might be right! During the years I was seeking answers for myself I explored many traditions and tried out many new ideas, to see what might work for me. I had many challenging thoughts and feelings, many confusing thoughts and feelings, and wanted to try to understand them better. So I kept seeking answers for myself.

Over the years, I've had various animals show up in my life, in various ways and with different levels of permanency. I see a lot of foxes, and the things that fox stands for does make sense to me in relation to my life. Just the other night a fox ran up the hill ahead of me as I drove home to the farm. Yet fox is not *always* with me. Other animals come and go in my life as well. If they show up, I read what they stand for and represent, and see how that applies to my life at that time. I take the lessons and I try to learn from them. All nature, all of this world, has lessons to teach us.

Go deeply into what you feel led to. Dive deep into study, prayer, meditation. Go deeply into spirit connections with like-minded others. For those of us who are emotionally wired, I believe our spirit life is vital to our happiness and contentment. Heart-centered people like us need to have things that make our souls sing and hum with life.

My deep dog Max

Let me share some very deeply personal, emotional things. When I was in my twenties, I got a dog. I had always been interested in Shar Peis, a very wrinkled Chinese breed, and my mom had seen a picture of one at a nearby shelter. She told me about him and I went to take a look at him, and adopted him immediately. His name was Max. He was a good dog and I loved him from day one, but I never really knew if he cared about me very much. He never showed any great attachment to me, or to anyone. Time passed, and the marriage I was in at the time had fallen apart. I was in a dark pit of depression and despair. One night, at my lowest moment, I decided I would kill myself. I didn't know exactly how, I didn't know exactly when, but I decided I would do it. I was tired of hurting. I felt like I couldn't take it anymore. While I sat on the floor crying out my suffering, Max came over to me. He lay down beside me and leaned hard against me. He never left me as I cried. I could hardly believe it. He had never shown any attachment to me at all. But somehow he knew how much I was hurting that night, and he was there for me. In that moment, I decided I had to live to take care of Max. I was afraid that no one else would be there for him but me, so I had to find a way to keep going.

I had him for many years; sixteen to be exact. After that night, he was firmly attached to me. He never left my side. He followed me everywhere I went. He loved me very deeply and I knew it. I didn't want to ever let him go. As he got older, I knew he was having some health issues. He began to have kidney problems, so I put him on a special diet. He was doing okay, but not great, and I just didn't want to face that. I was not ready to let him go.

One day he snapped at a little girl who patted him on the back. I knew then that he was in pain, that he was suffering, and I knew that I needed to let him go soon. It was such a hard decision. Even now, I'm crying as I write. I arranged with a veterinarian friend to bring Max to her on a Sunday to have him put down. After she sedated him, she said that based on his thickened skin condition, he probably was in a lot of pain and had been for a while. While this certainly confirmed for me that I was doing the right thing for him, it didn't stop the coming pain and grief.

I missed him so much. It hurt me terribly that he wasn't there. Night after night, I cried myself to sleep. I begged him to become one of my spirit guides. I wanted that so much. I didn't feel him around me, which added to my grief.

Months later at a zoetic meditation weekend retreat, I became aware of Max's spirit. We were doing a visualization exercise, and part of the imagery that I experienced was of me walking down a hallway of intense fear and suffering, a hall of death, it felt like to me. I had to get to the end of the hallway, but I knew I couldn't do it on my own. In that moment, I felt Max on my left side. I was able to grab his collar and he led me down that hallway. He got me through that exercise.

And he's been with me ever since. Feeling his spirit through the years has been a huge source of comfort to me.

Is this all nonsense? Is it just me creating things for myself? Maybe. Or is it real? Maybe. I know what I've experienced is real for me. I know the sensing of animal spirits around me, as well as my two angels spirits, have been of great comfort and support to me whenever I've gone through difficult life changes.

My Goddess Experiences

My belly dancing teacher, Karima, hosts an amazing ceremony every January, in which she honors the Goddess, and chooses a patron Goddess for the upcoming year. When she first talked to me about this many years ago, I was intrigued and so attended a ceremony. When I picked the name of a Goddess for the coming year, I knew nothing about her. Later when I was able to do some research, I was quite amazed! The story of this Goddess matched my whole life story up to that time….interesting. Over the next several years, I continued to attend Karima's yearly ceremony, choosing a new Goddess for each new year, and then researching who she was and how what she stood for might be relevant to me that year. What I found, either by chance or design, was the Goddess I chose (or who chose me!) consistently represented things I ended up needing to learn or understand that year. It became a very special practice for me to incorporate that female spirit, that female power, into my life in a more conscious way.

As I explored this female Goddess energy, I became aware of a workshop on human relationships called *Cuddle Party* (through a late night TV show, no less!) I checked into it, and it was real! I contacted the local facilitator, only to discover that she was a licensed social worker too. I took a deep breath, gathered my fears, and signed up to attend my first cuddle party.

It was nerve wracking for introverted me to be in a room full of pajama clad strangers. The welcome circle and a series of exercises during the first hour of the event helped put me at ease. In the welcome circle, the rules are shared. (Yes, there are rules for cuddling!) Some of these included, If you were a yes to a request, say *yes*; if you were a no, say *no*. If you were a maybe, say *no*. What fabulous guidelines to live by! You never *have* to cuddle anyone at a cuddle party. You never have to do anything you don't want to do. Again, an amazing rule to live by! Also, you never touched anyone at a cuddle party without making a verbal request and receiving verbal consent. If everyone in the real world followed this rule, we could eliminate so much pain and suffering!

These workshops helped me greatly to improve my communication skills and practice making connections with other people on many levels. It became a safe, structured, non-sexual way to get my human touch needs met while I was separated and not ready to date. Some of my dearest friends today I met at a cuddle party.

Edie Weinstein is the dear soul who facilitated my first and many of my subsequent cuddle parties. She is a great teacher, speaker, and writer. She was very encouraging to me as I wrote this book. Through Edie I became aware of an amazing teacher and healer named Amy Storm. And no, we're not related! I learned that Amy was doing a summer women's retreat, a Goddess retreat in New Jersey. I checked into it and decided to attend. I was quite nervous heading there, having never met Amy and only knowing Edie from the cuddle parties. It turned out to be an amazing experience.

Appreciation Exercise

One of the group exercises we did during the retreat was called *appreciation*. For this exercise, we all sat in a circle. The woman being appreciated stood in the middle. One by one each of us would share from our heart something about who she was to us, and what she means to us. This could go on for quite a long time. The first retreat I went to we spent hours and hours doing this for one another. At the beginning of this exercise, our leader, Amy, used metal dowsing rods, which measure energy. The rods gave her an approximate size of the participant's energy field. Before any appreciations were spoken, the rods showed that the woman's energy field was about two feet around her. After two or three people had spoken their words of love and appreciation to her, Amy would recheck her personal energy field with the rods. The energy field had expanded by many feet. After a few more appreciations, the energy field was even bigger than the room we were in. It was an amazing process to witness. And being in the middle of a circle of love, with so many beautiful and amazing things being spoken to you, is an experience I will never forget.

Oh, how we need to speak our hearts! How often do we feel alone and like no one cares? We need to practice speaking our hearts to all of the people in our lives who matter to us. We are not promised tomorrow; we never know how much time we truly have with anyone in this world. We need to let them know we care. Practice doing this today, for even just one person. It will bless them. And it will bless you.

Chapter 8

Purpose

What is your purpose? Do you know? Do you want to know? Do you feel you need to know? I struggled with this question a lot growing up. I've struggled with this question for much of my life, if I'm honest. I always felt like there was something big and important I was supposed to do, but I just couldn't figure out exactly what it was. This not figuring out my purpose caused me a great deal of stress for a very long time!

Do I know my purpose in life now? I know the big ones. I'm here in life now for two very clear reasons. I'm here to be a therapist. How I feel when I'm working with clients absolutely resonates with me. It makes my heart and soul sing. It's deeply satisfying to me. My other clear purpose is to be mom to my son Luke. We are soulmates.

Critters are vital to me. Cavies make me happy. My pet bunnies bring me joy. My human associations through the cavies are very important to me; they have become a second family to me.

I often feel little direction and little certainty about the details of the rest of my life. I have often felt without roots, without a home. I imagine I may not be the only one.

My lifelong struggle with purpose and identity became clearer to me when life coach Deborah Donndelinger introduced me to something called *human design* about seven years ago. She had been working with me using EFT to address some of my personal issues. She began to talk to me about this new thing she was learning and wanted to share with me. For several months I resisted it. I wouldn't give her my personal information in order for her to run my chart and tell me about my human design. But I finally relented and gave her the info she had requested. What followed in our next session was nothing short of amazing to me.

My Human Design

In our next session, she began to explain to me how I think, how I feel, how I process life, how I approach problems. She mentioned some ongoing issues I might have due to the specifics of my own personal human design. Though I don't remember many of the details she spoke to me that first time, what I do remember is literally saying to her over and over again things like, *How do you know this?!? I have struggled with that all my life! I have always felt that way! That issue has always been very hard for me.* She simply told me that all this information was in my human design chart.

I was hooked. I had to know more about this. I was getting more information about myself than I had ever gotten in my life from any kind of personality test or anything I had studied. I went online, ordered the manual, and dove an.

Note: I came to find out that my approach to this new information was totally in harmony with my design profile. I'm a 1/3 - which means I must dig down to the very rock bottom and learn everything there is to know about something to feel satisfied. I'm a big researcher. It also means that I must experience things for myself. I truly cannot learn much from the experiences of others. This explains a lot of my patterns in life.

I also learned that I'm a generator. As a generator, the proper strategy in life for me is to wait and respond. This isn't how I had conducted much of my life prior to this. I had very much taken in the social message of *just do it.* While this may be a correct strategy for some, this is not a proper strategy for generators. I had to learn to wait, to be patient, and only then respond to life. This was very hard for me at first.

Part of what makes it so difficult for me to wait has to do with some of my other internal wiring. I am emotionally defined, which means I have a defined solar plexus. This translates to my having set ways of being and feeling emotionally. My emotions run on a wave pattern, so at certain times I'm up; but at other times I'm down. This often has little to do with life events, and it's not bipolar disorder. Being emotionally wired means we experience ongoing shifts in our emotional lives that are normal for us.

I learned that I'm what is called a *triple split*. This means that the different defined centers in my personality system are not all connected. When there are splits in your system, you need other people or time to bridge these gaps and to process information in order to be able to make good decisions. As a triple split, there's no one human being who can bridge those gaps for me. I need many different kinds of people in my life to give me different input and experiences in order for me to be able to process life well. I also very much need time to be able to determine what the best decisions for me are.

My design also has a defined spleen, which means I have immediate knowledge and wisdom in the present moment about what to do and what actions to take. This can cause some natural conflict with the parts of my system that need time. As I began to study all of this, Deborah explained to me how my design had some parts that work very quickly, and other parts and aspects that needed more time. In order to do the very best for myself, I needed to learn to honor *all* the parts of my system. This made a great deal of sense to me, and explained much about my life. I am a mix.

Human design states that it takes about seven years of working with your design and coming to understand how best to operate, before you're at your optimum strength and at your very best. 2016 is my seventh year since I began working with my human design. I don't think it's an accident that it's now when this book became a reality.

Human design teaches that there is no good or bad design. Yet when we look at our design, we often have conditioned reactions to what we see. When I first looked at my design, what upset me greatly was my open identity center. While having this open identity center explains *SO* many things in my life, I still felt like it was a bad thing. When you have an open identity center, it means you have no fixed identity. People with undefined identity centers often gets stuck trying to find direction and love in their lives. These issues have absolutely ruled my life. They have driven me, and often not in very constructive ways. An open identity center allows me to experience just who my clients are; who anyone truly is. It can be an amazing experience. I have no *me* to get in the way.

The first year or two working with my own design, I continued to be very upset about my open identity center. I felt like this was a big problem; I feared it meant I would never be happy, that I would never know who I was. But over the years I have come to a greater acceptance of this aspect of my design. Yet there are still times I struggle with it. I'm having some struggles at this very moment with this part of my design.

The vital issue is to come to understand yourself in the best way possible for *YOU*. Find systems that work for you as you quest to understand and really grasp yourself. Work a program that helps you to come to peace with who you are, and how you can best operate at this time. Human design has helped me come to greater peace and acceptance of myself, but it may not be for you. Be curious – do some research – find what resonates with you.

Your Purpose

So, what *is* your purpose?

I truly believe it doesn't matter exactly what you do in this life and world. We need good people in all fields and from all walks of life. We need people with values and ethics and compassion everywhere on this planet. What matters is to find something that touches your heart, that blesses you, and that blesses other people.

I encourage people to follow their strengths, to follow their interests, to follow their passions. What we do for a living takes up a fair amount of our time; if you can enjoy what you do for work, all the better. If you enjoy what you do, you'll do it better. You'll be more successful and enjoy more of the rewards of your success.

Our purpose is about who we *are*, not what we *do*. So many of us get caught up in *doing* instead of *being*. We too often think our value is in what we accomplish. While it's fine to set goals and to get things done, just know that what you do, isn't *you*. Our ability to do things changes as we age. Over time, there will be things you simply *can't* do anymore. This loss of activity doesn't have to equal loss of identity.

This takes me back to the section on spirit. Our *true* identity comes from our soul and spirit. To be healthy, we need to be grounded in the essence of who we are. This is what lasts for always.

Personal Protection

There is no way to be 100% safe in this world. Accidents happen - people get sick – and sometimes very bad things happen. Trauma survivors can have an especially difficult time feeling safe. They know firsthand how bad things can get. Our goal is to learn how to help ourselves feel safer. We can take concrete action to feel more secure. Knowing this already helps our brains to relax. And a less stressed brain works better.

I like to envision a force field around me that extends about two to three feet. I imagine that this force field prevents hurtful and difficult things from reaching my heart. It doesn't change my awareness of what's going on around me; it just helps reduce the emotional intensity and its impact on me.

If I'm dealing with a difficult person or situation, I imagine their words or negative energy bouncing off of my force field. This helps keep me calm and in touch with the more logical part of my brain. That doesn't mean that I don't have feelings about them; I may be having a huge emotional reaction on the inside. What it does mean, however, is that I'm aware enough that I can try to keep my reactive feelings out of the situation. There may be times when it's appropriate to express your feelings. In those cases, go for it. But I would advise that you think carefully about who you're dealing with first, and then express yourself in a way that will more likely register with them, based on their personality.

Thinking about people who care about you is also a helpful practice for feeling less vulnerable. Our brains don't know the difference between a vividly imagined activity and what is happening in real life. That's why mental rehearsal works so well for performers, for athletes, well...for anyone! When we vividly imagine an event, our brains believe it is happening. So thinking about a time when someone you cared for was really there for you, will help you feel loved, which causes your brain to relax. It triggers all your positive limbic reactions. We can also imagine that someone we care about who's no longer here on earth is still here for us today. That can be just as powerful.

We can also call upon our own strong parts. This could be the badass part of you that probably doesn't get out much, but is still in you. It could be the tough, no nonsense business person part of you. Another strong part could be the mother or parent part, which will tirelessly defend any child. We all have various strong parts within us, but we may have to practice calling on them when we need them. Act as *if*. We all have different aspects to ourselves within that we can learn to call on at will; most of the time, we're simply not used to doing it.

If you're having a hard time identifying the parts of yourself that are strong, you can begin by incorporating external images of strength into your imagining. This could be a person you know in real life whose strength you admire. You might envision a superhero you like. Some people find that an image of spirit as they know it is safe feeling imagery for them. When I was a child, I often imagined Jesus was with me. This was a great source of comfort and strength for me.

We are all stronger and better than we know. We all have more resources available to us than we tap into. I believe that as children of the Divine we each have all kinds of abilities, we just need to learn how to best utilize them.

Neutrality

I used to think that to feel neutral would be unacceptable to me. But over the past few years I've gradually gotten to a more neutral place in my emotional life. My ups and downs are less extreme. This is partly due to the various mental practices I use routinely, to EFT, and to the medication I take when I need it. Being in a neutral state more often helps me to do life better and be more consistently productive.

Equanimity is defined as evenness of mind under stress. I hear balance implied in this definition. I also hear that being non-reactive is healthier. To me, it means to remain neutral. When we're in an emotionally neutral state, I believe we're best able to respond rather than react. Being highly emotional in our actions doesn't really help us deal better with the world.

We can still feel all of our feelings, but it doesn't do us good to stay stuck on them or to act from that place. I've learned to let myself feel it all, feel it deeply, but then to let it go; at least mostly. Emotional remnants may remain in me, but they no longer control me.

Johari Window

The *Johari Window* was created by two American psychologists, Joseph Luft and Harrington Ingham. Its purpose is to help people understand themselves better. In this group exercise, people are asked to describe themselves and others using various adjectives. There are four rooms or windows. One room or window represents what is known to self, and what is known to others. This is called the *arena*. A second room or window represents what is known to others, but not known to self. This is called the *blind spot*. A third room or window represents what is not known to others, but is known to self. This is labeled the *façade*. The fourth room or window represents what is not known to others, and not known to ourselves. This is called the *unknown*. As people see how they label themselves, and how other people might label them, there is insight and possible growth.

It's very common for us to see ourselves differently than others do. Many of us are much harder on ourselves than other people. Many of us don't see the good in us as easily as others do.

In *Buddha's Brain*, the authors talk about for areas of competence. To me this parallels the windows or the four rooms of the Johari Window. In this model the first stage of change or growth is called *unconscious incompetence*. This when we are blissfully ignorant. Putting it simply, we don't know that we don't know.

The second stage of change is called *conscious incompetence*. This is the hardest stage because we're aware that we don't know something or that we lack a skill. This is the most emotionally challenging place in the growth process. This is the stage where many people give up.

The third stage of change is called *conscious competence*. In this stage, we have a growing knowledge or ability but we must intentionally use it. It takes conscious effort to use the new skill or knowledge. This can be very hard. Some people may quit here as they don't like all the work it takes.

The fourth stage of change is called *unconscious competence*. This is the stage where the new skill or information becomes second hand, becomes natural to us. It takes very little or no effort at all to utilize that information or skill. This is also called mastery.

Give Yourself The Best Chance

Learning is a process. New abilities are a process. It is important to keep this in mind so that you remain patient with yourself as you develop new skills, new practices, and new abilities. I've read that it takes ten-thousand hours of effort to become a master at something. This means five years of full time, forty hours a week effort to actually become an expert. While this idea is being challenged by some, there's a good point to be made. Few people are prodigies. Most of us need time and much practice to become skilled at something. How often do we pick up a new hobby or endeavor, and after just a few weeks or months we quit. We truly don't give ourselves a chance. We need to look at everything in life as a long term project; life is a marathon, not a sprint.

Robert Spitzer, of the cavy world, wrote an article years ago about the five year plan. In his article he discussed how people are often impatient when acquiring animals and wanting to have big show winners right away. He talks about the value of finding good foundation stock, and breeding it rather than just showing it. Over a period of five years you'll develop your own strong herd and thus have quality animals to exhibit.

I read this many years ago, and think that it applies to just about anything we may be interested in. It may not take five years for you to achieve that goal you want, but it might. If you plan for five years and it only takes you three, great! You'll feel awesome and accomplished. If you plan for a year and it takes you two, you probably won't make it to the second year. It's about our expectations. We want to set ourselves up for success, not for failure.

Life is hard. Life can break our hearts. People can break our hearts. Our human life can tear at our souls. We don't need to make it any harder on ourselves. Let's stack the deck in our own favor for once!

Chapter 9

Putting It All Together

Thank you for joining me on this journey. I hope it's been helpful to you. I hope it's been encouraging to you. I know that things can get better for you, so I want to leave you with a few more ideas to deepen your understanding.

Neurons That Fire Together, Wire Together

Let's return to the brain for a moment. Our brain cells are always growing and re-growing. In *Buddha's Brain,* the authors share a brain functioning process which astonishes me. They explained that our minds actually recreate memories, so that each time we remember a memory, we actually create it again, in slightly different ways. All minds do this.

This brain reality can be used for our healing. If we have upsetting memories, we can shift them. As we bring up that old memory, we can connect it with more positive, soothing experiences in the present moment. By doing this we can shift feelings from past experiences, and make them different, better. We can color an old memory in a better light.

As I reread this, I realized that this was the answer to why we should be kind to ourselves! This reframing brain process is exactly why we need to practice self-compassion. If each time we remember a memory we judge it harshly, we make our past pain even worse for ourselves. If we choose to remember those experiences with a little kindness and compassion, we'll make the past a little lighter and a little easier to live with.

The fact that the brain recreates memories each time they're recalled also explains in part why EFT works. When we tap we're calling up a past experience or a feeling that's painful or uncomfortable. In doing this in a self-supporting way, we're able to shift the tone and feeling of that past bad experience or negative emotion.

Also, when we do EFT, we're bringing a self-soothing state to bear on a past memory that's upsetting or disturbing. This present moment self-soothing helps to shift the intensity of that memory. As neuroscience has shown, it actually *changes* the memories stored in the brain. After a while, the memories we carry will no longer be as emotionally charged. I've seen this work for me and many others.

Our Negativity Bias

Remember the negativity bias? Recall that our brains are wired for negativity, for noticing the abnormal, or the dangerous. In one sense, this represents a neurological imbalance. Our brains in a natural state are not actually balanced. Choosing to focus on the positive or better parts of our experiences actually serves to correct this negativity bias.

Choosing to be positive can be seen as simply working towards become a balanced human being. It serves to help us balance our mental scales. I teach this simple truth to my clients. They're usually experts at finding things that can go wrong. I ask them instead to begin to take notice of what could go right.

In her book on self-compassion, author Kristin Neff talks about how negative emotions narrow our attention. This causes us to make more mistakes. She also points out that positive emotions actually broaden our attention, so we can maximize our thinking and coping skills. That's another reason to focus on the good in life. It helps us become our best.

Desire, Craving, Suffering

Desire is not really the problem. We can want all day long. We can wish for more or different morning, noon, and night. Desire alone does not cause our suffering. Our *craving* is what causes suffering. Our intense craving for something in particular is what causes us to suffer.

When we crave something, we are very, very close to it. Frankly, we've become obsessed with it. That's what takes it from a desire to a craving. It's not healthy to grasp at things. We need a little space around our life experiences both good and bad. Space is what gives us the ability to be objective, and thus to make good choices.

All these different techniques I've shared with you are designed to allow you to gain some space and thus perspective from your issues and problems. With perspective and space, we can make better choices. That will break the chains of craving.

Savoring

One final idea for taking better care of yourself; it's something that Kristen talks about in her book on self-compassion. She calls it *savoring*. To do this, you consciously choose to focus on anything good about an experience you're having in the present moment. Intentionally intensify any good aspects, good feelings, and good images. By doing this, you magnify the positive aspects of the experience in your memory.

I practiced this on a recent trip to California to judge cavies. I arrived early to do some sightseeing, and was taken to the Monterey Bay Aquarium. It was an amazing place. I made it a point as I was walking through the beautiful exhibits to really focus on being present. Yes, I took lots of pictures (until my phone died!), but I also took the time to really feel what it was like to be there. I did what I could to imprint this experience into my memory bank. And even now, if I think about the different exhibits, I immediately feel how I felt there; peaceful, content, and present. It was a really good experience because I chose to make it more positively intense.

Conclusion

Let's review.

SAD

- STOP
- Adjust
- Do *You*

Stop tools include:

- Literally stop. Do/say nothing
- Physically relax
- Breathing methods
- Wet noodle
- Progressive muscle relaxation
- Pets
- EFT

Adjust tools include:

- Accept our feelings
- Affiliate with others like us
- The Work/Inquiry
- Stop people pleasing

- Self Compassion
- GEMS (Ruby, Pearl, Emerald, Sapphire)
- Adjusting your expectations of people and situations

Do You tools include:

- Spirit identity
- Prayer/Meditation
- Personal Passions
- Relationships
- Self care
- Coloring books
- Gratitude
- Medication
- Get physical
- Appreciation exercise
- Find a purpose (or more than one!)
- Personal protection (force field)
- Strong parts
- Savoring

I invite you to join me on my Facebook page called *SAD No More*. I will continue to remind you of your worth and value, and build you up. I will encourage and uplift you. We will review all these ideas on an ongoing basis. I also plan to post various videos of different healing techniques as I learn and practice new things. We can continue this healing journey together, as a heart-centered community.

From My Heart To Yours

Let me speak some words to you, to your heart. Listen and soak them in.

You are an amazing child of the Divine. You came from the stars. You are so beautiful. You are beautiful in Mind and Spirit. You are also beautiful in whatever human form you have taken. We are all differently shaped and that is ok. Maybe it's even wonderful.

Your heart….your kind, compassionate heart makes you so special and so valuable to this world. Some will not recognize the incredible worth of your heart. Some will ridicule you. Some will call you weak. They have no idea how very strong you are.

You have been through *SO* much. You have *FELT* so much. All of it is held in your deep, amazing heart. You gather things in your heart – feelings, people, experiences – and you ponder them. Let us keep learning how to do that in a way that nurtures us and build us up. Let us keep learning how to be good caretakers of our own hearts.

The world needs us, now more than ever. The hurting world and the hurting beings in it need us. The world needs us strong and at our very best. This human life is very challenging.

We do our healing for ourselves but also for the world. Remember that. All you do for yourself *IS* to help others, truly. Healing is never selfish, in a final sense. The more you do for yourself that is positive, the more you can do for others. We can learn to thrive, not just exist, in this world. That is what I wish for each of you.

I hope we can meet one another someday. And when we do, I hope I can give you a big, long hug. I love hugs. I bet many of you do as well. I'm here for you. Let's be here for each other.

Resources

A general theory of love by Thomas Lewis, MD, Fari Amini, MD, Richard Lannon, MD

Animal Speak by Ted Andrews

Buddha's Brain: the practical neuroscience of happiness, love and wisdom by Rick Hansen, PhD with Richard Mendias

Codependent No More by Melody Beattie

Gabrielle Ross

GEMS created by Dani Johnson (website – www.danijohnson.com)

Hypothalamus and HPA defined by Wikipedia

Johari window created by Joseph Luft and Harrington Ingham

Limbic system: amygdala by Anthony Wright, PhD, UT medical school at Houston

Liora Hill (website – www.zoeticworkshops.azurewebsites.net)

Loving What Is by Byron Katie

Merriam-Webster Dictionary

The Secret by Rhonda Byrne

Self compassion by Kristin Neff

Self parenting: the complete guide to your inner conversations by John K. Poland

The ten core competencies of trauma, PTSD, grief and loss, training by Eric Gentry, PhD, LMHC

Weight Management Psychology online course

Wikipedia

Made in the USA
Middletown, DE
19 September 2016